ALL YOU EVER WANTED
TO KNOW FROM HIS HOLINESS

THE

DALAI
LAMA

ON HAPPINESS,
LIFE, LIVING, and
MUCH MORE

HAY HOUSE TITLES OF RELATED INTEREST

YOU CAN HEAL YOUR LIFE, the movie,
starring Louise L. Hay & Friends
(available as a 1-DVD program and an expanded 2-DVD set)
Watch the trailer at: **www.LouiseHayMovie.com**

⊕　⊕

*COMMIT TO SIT: Tools for Cultivating a Meditation Practice
from the Pages of Tricycle,* edited by Joan Duncan Oliver

*FOLLOWING SOUND INTO SILENCE:
Chanting Your Way Beyond Ego into Bliss* (book-with-CD),
by Kurt (Kailash) A. Bruder, Ph.D., M.Ed.

THE GURU OF JOY: Sri Sri Ravi Shankar & the Art of Living,
by François Gautier

CHANTS OF A LIFETIME, by Krishna Das
(book-with-CD; available November 2009)

*IN MY OWN WORDS: An Introduction to My Teachings and
Philosophy,* by His Holiness the Dalai Lama; edited by Rajiv Mehrotra

*A NEW WAY OF THINKING, A NEW WAY OF BEING: Experiencing
the Tao Te Ching,* by Dr. Wayne W. Dyer (available August 2009)

UNDERSTANDING THE DALAI LAMA, edited by Rajiv Mehrotra

YOGA, POWER, AND SPIRIT: Patanjali the Shaman,
by Alberto Villoldo, Ph.D.

YOUR SOUL'S COMPASS: What Is Spiritual Guidance?
by Joan Borysenko, Ph.D., and Gordon Dveirin, Ed.D.

⊕　⊕

All of the above are available at your
local bookstore, or may be ordered by visiting:

Hay House USA: **www.hayhouse.com**®
Hay House Australia: **www.hayhouse.com.au**
Hay House UK: **www.hayhouse.co.uk**
Hay House South Africa: **www.hayhouse.co.za**
Hay House India: **www.hayhouse.co.in**

ALL YOU EVER WANTED
TO KNOW FROM HIS HOLINESS

THE
DALAI
LAMA

ON HAPPINESS,
LIFE, LIVING, and
MUCH MORE

Conversations with Rajiv Mehrotra

HAY HOUSE, INC.
Carlsbad, California • New York City
London • Sydney • Johannesburg
Vancouver • Hong Kong • New Delhi

Published and distributed in the United States by: Hay House, Inc.: www.hayhouse.com • **Published and distributed in Australia by:** Hay House Australia Pty. Ltd.: www.hayhouse.com.au • **Published and distributed in the United Kingdom by:** Hay House UK, Ltd.: www.hayhouse.co.uk • **Published and distributed in the Republic of South Africa by:** Hay House SA (Pty), Ltd.: www.hayhouse.co.za • **Distributed in Canada by:** Raincoast: www.raincoast.com • **Published in India by:** Hay House Publishers India: www.hayhouse.co.in

Editorial supervision: Jill Kramer • *Design:* Tricia Breidenthal

Library of Congress Cataloging-in-Publication Data

Bstan-'dzin-rgya-mtsho, Dalai Lama XIV, 1935-
  All you ever wanted to know from His Holiness the Dalai Lama on happiness, life, living, and much more : conversations with Rajiv Mehrotra. -- 1st ed.
    p. cm.
  ISBN 978-1-4019-2018-0 (hardcover)
  1. Bstan-'dzin-rgya-mtsho, Dalai Lama XIV, 1935---Interviews. 2. Buddhism--Miscellanea. I. Mehrotra, Rajiv, 1953- II. Title.
  BQ7935.B774A76 2009
  294.3'420423--dc22

                                      2008037880

ISBN: 978-1-4019- 2018-0

12   11   10   09   4   3   2   1
1st edition, February 2009

Printed in the United States of America

This book is dedicated . . .

*To all sentient beings
that we may together find happiness
and avoid suffering*

*To the many spiritual masters
who with infinite patience
and deep compassion
have so generously given of
their insights and wisdom
to a most unworthy aspirant*

*And in particular to
His Holiness the Dalai Lama
&
B. K. S. Iyengar
Late Swami Ranganathananda
Late Baba Amte*

CONTENTS

INTRODUCTION

The Dalai Lama stands tall at the ethical and moral center of an interdependent globalized world, because in all that he does, represents, and embodies, he reconciles seeming contradictions with remarkable ease. In pursuing the human rights of the Tibetan people and the preservation of their culture, His Holiness seeks not political independence—not even as a negotiating position—but genuine autonomy and a commitment to working together with the "great Chinese people." He is a religious leader, believed by millions to be an incarnation of the Buddha, yet one who delights in recounting his frailties, one who counsels caution to those abandoning their faith, even when they may be converting to his own. A passionate activist for the interfaith movement, he is also a doctor of metaphysics who vigorously pursues a dialogue with modern science and works hard to learn from it.

The Dalai Lama must ultimately succeed in his many strivings if we are to believe in the ultimate triumph of all that he embodies—all that is good, true, and just.

The printed word can never be a substitute for listening to the many levels at which His Holiness communicates and the impact that his words can have on our own understanding, beyond their formal meaning in any dictionary. This is even so when he speaks in what he describes as his "bad English," often turning to his formal interpreter or personal secretary for confirmation that he is using the right word. When he speaks in Tibetan, explaining a complex idea that needs to be translated, he doesn't passively accept the offered translation and frequently intervenes to suggest a better or more accurate rendering.

He has the uncanny ability to respond to a question or engage in a conversation at the level of the other person's understanding. When he is unable to respond in this manner or when he genuinely believes he doesn't have an answer, there is no hesitation in simply saying, "I don't know."

Nothing other than being in his presence can give anyone a sense of his profound humanity; his deep, resonating laughter; his infectious joy and gentle humor . . . the unceasing flow of a calm, reassuring, and warm energy that no transcript can capture.

The Dalai Lama listens and talks to all kinds of people. Many wait patiently for hours, weeks—even years—for a few moments with him. He approaches each conversation with patience, concentration, and great respect for the other person. Whether those he encounters are part of a lineup of new arrivals from Tibet, who have often risked their lives to reach Dharamsala just for a glimpse of him, or everyday people he runs into in hotel lobbies, elevators, sidewalks, and airplanes as he travels around the globe; whether they are veteran politicians or experienced journalists, novice monks or nervous interns, scientists or philosophers, atheists or men or women of deep faith, beggars on the street or business tycoons in mansions—for the Dalai Lama, they are all human beings, each of whom wants happiness and wants to avoid suffering.

This book of conversations with His Holiness represents an articulation of his insights and perspectives recorded and documented over more than 25 years. I have been deeply blessed and privileged to have been a personal student of his during what seems only a brief moment in the timeless eternity I feel I have known him. While our meetings were usually one-on-one conversations, some were with larger groups, and a few were recorded for my long-running television program *In Conversation* on Doordarshan, the national public-service broadcaster in India.

Most of the early conversations were private journeys with His Holiness in his personal chambers or the audience room in McLeod Ganj, India, where the Tibetan government in exile is headquartered. I initially scribbled down our exchanges upon returning to my room, once the rush of emotion and epiphany from time with him had settled and the intensity of the lived moments threatened to fade.

I felt that I needed to freeze every word, every moment, lest my memory let me down. There was no motive other than my own learning and understanding. Over the years, as technology became more easily available to me, I often used a tape recorder whenever the sessions with him were more formal or involved other people.

In none of the conversations did I represent or seek to present an objective, journalistic persona. The Dalai Lama has been my "guru" and I, an unworthy "chela"—to use the traditional Sanskrit terms. I use these words to acknowledge, especially in the context of this book, the intensity of my personal commitment to our relationship and to celebrate the generosity of spirit with which he has so often indulged me with his time, teachings, and wisdom.

I know the Dalai Lama would not approve of my uncritical attitude, but he would approve of my obligation to acknowledge the truth of it to myself and others. In the ancient tradition of the Buddha, the Dalai Lama has consistently urged that we not accept any philosophy or teacher purely on the basis of uncritical, unquestioning faith and surrender. While these may often be useful qualities in a spiritual context, they must be juxtaposed with reason and logic. His Holiness asks that we look at him, as with all things, in this spirit. He would ask, as I do, that such a spirit be applied to this book.

Typically during personal "audiences," there would be no one else present, making our conversations more intense and intimate. I deliberately use the word *conversations* because His Holiness is always deeply interested in the person he is talking to—in fact, in the everyday lives and predicaments of all people. That he found the time and genuine curiosity to listen to my inane trivia and respond to my questions is a tribute to his remarkable qualities of empathy, patience, and compassion. I hasten to reassure the reader that I have done my best to edit myself out of the text. I have also taken the liberty of reorganizing the material to try to ensure a more coherent, structured flow of ideas than my incoherent brain could evolve during the actual unfolding of the conversations.

The Dalai Lama's spontaneity is reflected in his style of speaking. As he speaks, his words draw upon the depths of personal knowledge, insights, and experience that he has acquired through the course of his life. He focuses on the integrity and clarity of his communication rather than obsessing with fluid sentence constructions. He rarely draws upon a programmed ordering of words or sentences from memory, even when he responds to questions he has addressed a thousand times before. Every sentence is a new personal discovery for him, a gesture of respect to the listener.

His Holiness seldom writes in English himself. The books and articles he has authored are usually translations of oral teachings or material dictated in Tibetan. His spoken English inevitably needs substantial editing for print. Given the diverse people who do this—and that includes different simultaneous interpreters—there is no consistent style or vocabulary that has been, or perhaps ever can be, evolved.

This inevitably leads to inconsistencies that can be disconcerting to a reader, the more so when they appear within the same book. I have tried to resolve these in some measure, but have not entirely succeeded. I have been especially reluctant to try to aggressively fine-tune those passages, particularly on the dharma, that were translated by His Holiness's interpreters. Of course, I remain responsible for any errors that remain.

As I prepare the final text for publication, the Dalai Lama has recently celebrated his 73rd birthday and is approaching his 50th year in exile. For him, it was just another day, but he did ask the Tibetan community and the many of us who celebrate him every day to rededicate ourselves to becoming better human beings, to develop real compassion and genuine altruism, to work toward diminishing our sense of our personal "self" so that we may better serve others. That, he said, would be the most gratifying birthday offering to him.

The future of Tibet seems grim. The special envoys of His Holiness have yet again returned from the seventh round of unproductive talks with the Chinese. The continuing triumph of Chinese military and economic power, the ides of March 2008—after long years of hopelessness—brought both cheer and despair. The widespread protests by Tibetans in China despite its government's Orwellian stranglehold and the demonstrations against the Olympic torch wherever it traveled in the free world are a reminder that the Tibetan cause is alive. It is begging our collective conscience to stand up to Chinese obduracy and bullying.

Ironically, it took images of violence carried on television screens around the globe to remind us of the singular power of a pacifist Buddhist monk. He has kept alive the cause of his people, while living in exile as a guest of a foreign government. He has done this with a deep commitment to nonviolence that is bred of a tradition that is as deceptively simple as the man himself.

Inspired by Mahatma Gandhi, for whom the means were more important than the ends, the Dalai Lama believes it is the motivation behind one's actions (and this includes violence) that is more important. He argues: "Violence is fundamentally wrong. But in some exceptional circumstances, with an altruistic motive, when there is no other alternative, one can consciously and with full awareness of the personal karmic consequences, commit such an act."

The Dalai Lama prays for the Chinese that "their veils of ignorance" might lift and asks us all—especially those Tibetans who are victims of Chinese oppression—to do so. He has disappointed tens of thousands of Tibetans, particularly the younger generation, by his refusal to support their violent protests against the Chinese inside Tibet (even as he understood their "frustration") and his unwillingness to endorse a boycott of the 2008 Olympics, which he felt the Chinese people were entitled to host.

A "Living Buddha," he responded with tears and over-whelming emotion while he sat with the prime minister of his elected government in exile as news of renewed violence in Tibet first trickled in. He does reassure us, how-ever, that given his years of Buddhist practice and train-ing, he was still able to distance himself enough from the unfolding present to get a good night's sleep.

He talks more often now of his imminent retire-ment; of the issues of succession; of his commitment to seeking rebirth in whatever form, manner, or place will provide the best context for him to serve humanity. As a Buddhist monk, a *bodhisattva,* this seeking is at the core of his aspiration. There will be another Dalai Lama if the situation requires one. The institution in itself is not important. What is vital is the future of the Tibetan peo-ple and the preservation of their ancient culture, which has nurtured among the most sophisticated techniques of mind training and the pursuit of real happiness. These belong to all humankind.

As I sign off the book to the publishers, I am reminded that true masters are those who have the courage to be intensely human, to acknowledge their frailties and their struggles, to constantly engage with them so that they can lift their own veils of ignorance, even as they urge others to do so for themselves. The Dalai Lama has the humility and the confidence to both embody and acknowledge this. These conversations assure us that his journey and accomplishments could yet be our own.

The following conversations
took place over a span of more than 25 years,
between 1982 and 2008.

Editor's note: In the dialogues that follow, questions posed by Rajiv Mehrotra will be in italics, and **HH:** will precede His Holiness the Dalai Lama's responses.

CHAPTER 1

RELIGION IN THE MODERN WORLD

Your Holiness, how important is religion in the modern world? Do we really need it?

HH: Religious influence is mainly at the individual level. Irrespective of one's faith or philosophy, transformation takes place within. In a way, that should give us hope. Materially, many have lost hope. However, at a deeper level, faith will sustain hope. Hope is a contributing factor for religion today. Once hope is lost, one becomes mad, commits acts of violence, participates in destructive behavior, or ultimately commits suicide.

Society is made up of individuals. Because of individuals who have lost hope and behave negatively, there is more and more madness in society today. If their numbers increase, all of society will suffer. If we utilize and understand religious traditions properly, individuals benefit, and so can society as a whole.

Unfortunately, religions today place too much emphasis on ceremony and rituals. This is sometimes old-fashioned and often limiting. What is necessary now is to find the essence of what is important in our daily lives and to connect relevant religious messages, advice, or inspiration with this.

I feel an important factor in religion is to be "God-fearing." Even though the individual believes he or she has individual power and faculties, a faith in God ensures there is some discipline. Many countries today face a moral crisis, and crimes are increasing. The disciplinary powers of society have conventional methods to control crime, but the individuals involved in wrongdoing are becoming more evasive and sophisticated in their methods. So without self-discipline, some acknowledgment of the spirit within one's self, and a sense of individual responsibility, it will be very difficult to exercise control. Therefore, various religious traditions have an important, effective role.

What would you say is the essential message of religion?

HH: I believe all major religions teach us to be more compassionate. All religions carry the message of love, compassion, and forgiveness. And forgiveness reflects tolerance and an understanding of the value of another's rights and views. This is the foundation for harmony.

Perhaps, at a deeper level, our views are transformed because of religious traditions. Religion teaches us some obvious things, but there are some deeper meanings, deeper forces, and deeper influences that it imparts. These widen our view of life. For instance, if an individual has to face pain or suffering, a religious experience or understanding will give deeper meaning to the incident and help reduce the mental burden, anxiety, and pain that are endured.

For example, Buddhists believe in the karmic law, the law of causality, so they know that whatever is happening in their lives is because of some past action, or karma. Ultimately, they know they must take responsibility for those actions. This helps to reduce mental frustration and anxiety.

Even if all religions have the same goal, there tend to be different ideas and areas of emphasis. As someone engaged purposefully in interfaith dialogue, how would you articulate the common ground or the basis for harmony between various religions?

HH: Although all world religions carry the message of love and compassion, it would not be correct to say that all of them have the same objective or beliefs; there are substantial differences. For example, some religions believe in a Creator, and others do not—that represents a fundamental difference.

There exist fundamental differences between the philosophical approaches of the world's religions. Why did all these diverse philosophies develop? I believe there is a good purpose for these multiple views. Within humanity, there are many different dispositions; and one philosophy, one belief, simply cannot satisfy all. Therefore, the great ancient masters had to demonstrate different philosophies and traditions.

For example, some like spicy food; others do not. Spirituality is food for the mind, and different religions

3

are very necessary for different mental dispositions. For some, the philosophy that the person is nothing and the Creator is most important is suitable. If everything is in the hands of the Creator, one should do nothing against the wishes of the Creator. If people act accordingly, it gives them a kind of mental satisfaction and moral stability. There are others who approach philosophy with logic. They have a sort of independence or some such power. If it is explained to them that everything is not in the hands of an Almighty Creator but is in their own hands, that really makes a difference.

Irrespective of the different philosophies, the most important point is to have a tamed and disciplined mind and a warm heart. It is unfortunate that today there is so much conflict, division, and bloodshed in the name of religion.

When I was in Tibet, there was no contact with other religious traditions. At that time, my thinking was different. Today, as a result of the many opportunities I have had to meet people from different religious traditions, I am completely convinced that they all have the same potential to produce good human beings. My eyes were opened after speaking with such great people as the late Thomas Merton, Mother Teresa, and so many more. We exchanged deep spiritual experiences, and I realized it is important to come together and work closely with each other.

As a Nobel laureate whose contribution toward secularism is especially lauded, what is your message on religious pluralism?

HH: In India, there are many different traditions of thought and philosophy, including the traditions of other cultures. India is like a supermarket of many religious traditions, and I think that is one of the beautiful things about this country. And because of that reality, religious *ahimsa* [the doctrine of refraining from harming any living being] has become a part of the Indian tradition. In this, India has set an example for the world. People can live side by side as brothers and sisters despite following many different religious faiths.

This is how the world is becoming smaller and so interdependent. In the past, nations and continents remained more or less isolated. The concept of one truth, one religion, was very relevant then. But today the situation is different. Pluralism in religious faith is necessary and relevant in today's world.

It is important for me as a Buddhist to believe that Buddhism is the true religion or one truth. It is just as important for a Christian to believe that Christianity is the true religion for him as it is for others. But how do we overcome the contradiction that there is relevance for different truths and traditions?

In reality, there is no contradiction. For the individual, the concept of one truth, one religion, is very important. However, in terms of society and the masses, the concept of several truths, several traditions, is relevant. I'm Buddhist, and I believe that Buddhism is the best. That does not mean that any one of my brothers— whether Hindu, Christian, Muslim, or Jewish—is following a religion of lesser validity. We are all involved in a religion that is appropriate for us.

Today we have the opportunity for closer contact with different traditions, which helps us develop the idea of pluralism and appreciate the values and sanctity of other customs. I learn many valuable things from other traditions. Similarly, some of my friends are also eager to learn from the Buddhist tradition. This is a healthy way to enrich one's own tradition and develop genuine mutual respect and admiration. I think that's a sound basis for religious harmony.

What is the Buddhist view of converting an individual from one faith to another? Today, in the West especially, there are many people of different faiths who have shown an interest in Buddhism. What advice would you give them?

HH: Conversion is one-sided when it is without alternatives and is coerced. This is wrong. Voluntary conversion is when an individual makes a choice according to his mental disposition. This seems more suitable to me. Sometimes disaster and confusion follow a change of religion, so it is safer and healthier, perhaps, for people to involve themselves in their own cultural traditions.

My advice to people who wish to convert: First, if one has to follow some faith, it is better to follow one's own traditional values or religion. Some Westerners who change their religion suddenly, without proper or careful thought, experience confusion. In case you find the Buddhist way or approach more effective and logical, think carefully. Time spent thinking and examining is worthwhile. Finally, if you really feel it is more suitable to your mental disposition, it is okay. An individual has the right to embrace a new religion.

And to digress a bit, when one changes one's personal religion, there is a tendency to be critical of the original religion in order to justify one's decision. That's very bad. It must be avoided. Buddhism may be more suitable for many, yet that does not mean that millions of other people have no values. Those millions do benefit from their religions.

Some practitioners of Buddhism have expectations that are too high, possibly because some of our teachers say that you can achieve Buddhahood within three years. Such a teaching is simply propaganda—you cannot achieve the highest spiritual realization in such a short period, except in exceptional cases. Too many expectations, in the beginning, are wrong. I myself think about the limitless eons that have given me inner strength. One hundred years of a life period is nothing.

Some practitioners cling to one practice without understanding the whole Buddhist system. The transformation of our mind cannot be achieved through just one effort or one practice. Our mind is both very weak and very strong, and it is very sophisticated. When your emphasis is more on learning, you may develop pride. If your emphasis is less on pride, sometimes you lose self-confidence. When you develop more self-confidence, pride also follows.

The mind is very sophisticated, so the antidote to it should also be sophisticated. Think about impermanence; think about eons; think about Buddha's nature, about the ultimate reality of emptiness; and also think about the mental potential. Think in various ways, and adopt different methods for different situations. That's the way to shape or change our mind. It takes time. For that reason it is very important to know the basic structure of the Buddhist practice. That's my advice or suggestion.

How does one discern which practice is best? For example, Buddhist practices depend much on logic, reasoning, and the mind. However, when there are "extraordinary" experiences, one might face a contradiction of sorts and want to dismiss them as "illogical."

HH: I think, in the beginning, you should simply think of different reasons or different methods that you feel are most effective. That is the only way to judge. Later, at a higher stage, I think that through dreams or sometimes through different kinds of unusual experiences, you can investigate different ways.

To give an explanation from tantra: We can infer certain experiences through the gross levels of our mind and others through the subtle mind. During sleep, in the dream state, our consciousness has reached a subtler level than during the waking state. This provides us with the opportunity to get a glimpse of certain experiences that are not possible during the waking state when the mind is active at grosser levels. Because of that, one can actually engage in certain investigations during the dream state. Therefore, one can also say that certain things exist that one can only understand through unusual experiences or experiences in dreams.

As I said earlier, all major religions have a single aim—to make good human beings. In this respect, they are the same. Beyond that, there are differences within the different spiritual traditions. One group—for example, Christians—believe that human beings ultimately reach Heaven. However, Buddhism, Jainism, and some ancient Indian traditions accept *nirvana, moksha*. Within Buddhism, there are different definitions and interpretations of moksha.

The main point is that among the systems that agree on the existence of nirvana and moksha, there are differences. Even among Buddhists, there are differences in the presentation of what is meant by nirvana. Buddhists explain nirvana as the true cessation of all delusions, a mind free of delusions. However, if we were asked whether other systems existed in which such a state could be achieved, the answer would have to be no. In the same way, if we Buddhists were asked if a Buddhist practice existed by which we could achieve going to Heaven—as Christians do—the answer would again have to be no.

A complete system of methods has to be practiced in order to achieve the state of nirvana as explained in Buddhism. There are many people who are not interested in practicing that type of path. There are many people to whom faith appeals more than reason.

Would it be correct to say that to those to whom logical reasoning and investigation appeal, Buddhism is the ideal complete path?

HH: I would agree. However, your question implies that Buddhist teaching presents the path in an exclusively logical way, but if we analyze this, it may not be immediately obvious.

There are different levels of direct experience and perception of both ultimate and relative truth that can be achieved through intense meditative and yogic practices. During the early stages, we can understand such experiences only by using logic and reasoning. We cannot experience them directly. There are only a few people who have had these deep, nuanced, and direct insights of the different levels of truth, for example.

Three types of phenomena exist: some are obvious, some slightly hidden, and others are completely hidden. For example, when we ask how this book came into existence, the usual explanation is that it was produced by causes and conditions. When we ask why it came into existence through such causes and how all these conditions and causes aggregate it, and then, if we delve further, we will come to the point where we will have to say that it was possible due to the karma of the person who has contact with this book. If we investigate even further in order to explain the book's existence, we might have to go as far as the big bang theory—the beginning of the universe.

The continuity of matter, even simple matter, goes like this, back to the previous stage, then to a stage before that stage, right to the beginning of the whole cosmos. The next question is: what is the reason for the creation of such things? Either God or some different instance is the answer. If the answer were the Creator God, it might solve one problem but create others, create more questions.

There is no beginning; this is endless because of sentient beings, because of the continuity of consciousness. That is the Buddhist explanation. This may not answer all the questions, but it answers some. This theory gives some satisfactory answers, which can be established through reasoning.

For example, certain facts cannot be proved, and we have to rely on the statements of a third person. We know that we are a certain number of years old, but we do not know this through our own experience, nor can we prove it through reasoning. We have to believe our mothers. We have faith in our mothers because there is no reason why they should lie. When we finally find that a person is completely reliable, we accept his or her statements. What is meant by reasoning or faith is to understand the consequences of certain actions that have accumulated over a certain period of time.

If we are to rely on the direct perceptions of a Buddha, we have to be convinced that the Buddha is free of ignorance and obscuration. We realize that there is no reason for him to tell lies and that the statements are not inconsistent and have no contradictions. When these conditions are fulfilled, we believe him and have faith in him.

CHAPTER 2

BUDDHISM

Your Holiness, Buddhism is a treasure that journeyed from India to Tibet. Tibet preserved it, and now you bring it back, not just to us Indians but to the entire world. What makes Buddhism distinct from other spiritual schools?

HH: The teachings of Buddha Shakyamuni can be divided into two categories: view and conduct. The conduct that Buddha taught is the behavior of *ahimsa*, nonviolence—not to harm. The practice of not harming others can be divided into two: first, to refrain from harming others; and second, to benefit them and work for their welfare.

This "nonharming" conduct has its root in the Buddha's being. If someone harms others, he acts against the wishes of the Buddha, but the reason for engaging in nonharming conduct has to be explained from the view of interdependent arising. This is central to the teachings of Buddhism.

It is said that the sufferings we do not wish and the happiness we desire and cherish are all products of mere causes. Besides that, there is no Creator. The ultimate Creator is one's own mind. The mind is intrinsically pure and good. With good motivation, the mind's verbal and physical actions are good and produce good results that are pleasant and beneficial.

On the other hand, when the mind remains untamed or becomes irritable, we commit harsh verbal and physical actions, which by nature harm or hurt others, and the result is unpleasant and painful. Ultimately, this is related to one's own mind. We cannot blame others for our suffering; we can only blame ourselves. The responsibility for it lies on our own shoulders. Buddhists, thus, believe in self-creation; there is no Almighty God or Creator.

From the point of view of nonviolence and compassion, all religions teach us to be good human beings, to have good motivation and good character. Good motivation and good behavior come from a warm heart.

On this point, all major world religions agree, don't they? The ways of approach, however, are different. Some religions teach the existence of God—God as Creator, we the created. Finally, things depend on God. If we act according to the wishes of God, we will achieve permanent happiness. The aim of all religions is more or less the same—to benefit all humanity. Realizing this is very important.

Buddhism is essentially a system of personal practice and personal evolution. There is the notion of the <u>bodhisattva,</u> which you embody. You symbolize the idea of engaged Buddhism, which means Buddhism engaged more with social

14

issues and phenomena, not just personal happiness. How does a system of philosophy that is basically geared toward personal transformation translate into a social reality?

HH: First, I never say that I am a bodhisattva. I am just a person who has a great desire to *become* a bodhisattva. But Buddhism was always actually engaged with society. The concepts of *dana* (generosity) and *shila* (ethical discipline) involve the other. The Mahayana way is heavily engaged with society. Dana means giving to others, not oneself. The three practices of shila—restraining from harmful action; cultivating, protecting, and increasing virtue; and helping and benefiting living things—all involve being engaged with the other, without neglecting one's own improvement.

I have always admired our Christian brothers and sisters, who are very devoted to God and at the same time are heavily engaged in social service, especially in the fields of education and health.

Your Holiness, please summarize for us the teachings of the Buddha and the Four Noble Truths for a beginner to Buddhism.

HH: The Buddha taught two groups of cause and effect. One is the group of cause and effect of delusions. For example, if the cause is bad action, the result is suffering. The other is the group of cause and effect equal to pure phenomena—that is, a virtuous cause and resultant happiness.

The First Truth is the truth of suffering, which is divided into three types of suffering:

— **First**, the suffering of suffering that is experienced by both human beings and animals.

— **Second**, the suffering of change, such as the suffering of hunger and thirst. We eat and drink to overcome this suffering, but if we go on eating and drinking, it can create other sufferings. This kind of suffering is the clear suffering experienced in the so-called developed countries. When people there get something new—a new camera, a television set, a new car—they are very happy. Very soon, however, that happiness diminishes, and the new article starts to give worries. They throw it away and want another one. We call this the suffering of change.

— The **third** type of suffering is the suffering of conditioning. Our physical form, the product of our own contaminated actions and delusions, is the main cause of this. Our own actions and delusions, and also our present form, produced our rebirth.

Release from the first two categories of suffering is not what is meant by *nirvana,* or liberation. When we sit here and feel comfortable, we are free of the first suffering, the suffering of suffering. But we are actually afflicted by the second type of suffering, the suffering of change.

There are people who, through the force of their *samatha* and *vipasyana* meditation, are able to go beyond the experience of the gross type of suffering and happiness and remain in a neutral state of mind. They are free from the first two kinds of suffering. Once these persons are also free from the third type of suffering, their aggregates—the product of contaminated actions and delusions—they achieve nirvana. These are the three categories of suffering of the First Noble Truth, the truth of suffering.

In order to find release from suffering, we must first eliminate the causes of suffering. The causes are within us. The second stage is to investigate the cause of suffering, and this is the Second Noble Truth, the truth of the cause of suffering. It says that all our happiness and suffering are caused by our own actions—by karma, the factor that induces the motivation of action.

The Third Noble Truth is the truth of the cessation of suffering. The means by which one accomplishes this is the path to cessation of suffering, the Fourth Noble Truth. But to begin, one has to think very carefully about whether suffering is something one can eliminate or not.

What is the fundamental philosophy and principle of Tibetan Buddhism?

HH: The religion known as Buddhism was taught by Buddha Shakyamuni. There are two major systems of Buddhism: *Mahayana,* the Greater Vehicle; and *Hinayana,* the Lesser Vehicle. Buddha Shakyamuni propounded the Hinayana system in public teachings, which were recorded. For obvious and specific reasons, the Mahayana teachings were only given to very exclusive groups of people. Mahayana teachings not only explain the techniques for training the mind but also for the penetration of vital points of the body. The latter are based on the physical body, and that part of the teachings is called *Tantrayana.*

There are two ways to teach the Buddha Dharma. One is the guru teaching the disciples; in some cases, there are prayers before the teachings begin. The other way, just like this one, is a completely informal discussion, not necessarily between guru and disciple.

Take, for example, myself. I have taken the *bhikshu* (mendicant) vows, according to the Vinaya Sutra, on which my daily way of life and conduct are based. I live as a monk. In our tradition, fully ordained monks observe 253 rules. We have to observe these rules. My daily practice of the development of *bodhicitta* [the state of mind of a bodhisattva], which is based on *karuna* and *maitri* [the perfect virtues of compassion and sympathy], is a practice of Mahayana teachings, so it is the main practice.

I also practice daily from the Vinaya Sutra—the essence of Hinayana teachings, including some practice of samatha and some of vipasyana. In addition, during the bodhicitta practice, I practice the six *paramitas* [perfections] as much as I can. We also practice deity yoga with mandalas, different kinds of forms.

So, one person—always at the same time, same place—practices these three teachings simultaneously. Buddhism in which all three systems are complete was preserved in the Tibetan community. Therefore, the practice of the essence of these three systems by the same person is a unique feature of Tibetan Buddhism.

How would you summarize the fundamental difference between the two primary schools—or rather, <u>vehicles,</u> as they are called—of Buddhism: <u>Mahayana</u> and <u>Hinayana?</u>

HH: According to the tradition of the Vaibhasika school—a Hinayana school—our kind Master Buddha Shakyamuni was an ordinary person at first. He cultivated the altruistic attitude of bodhicitta, engaged in the practice of the path, and eventually achieved enlightenment. If in the Mahayana system it was accepted that Buddha Shakyamuni was an ordinary human being before he achieved enlightenment during that lifetime, there would be some inconsistencies.

In the writings of the Hinayana system, certain differences are mentioned between the Master Buddha and the Sravaka and Pratyekabuddhas [religious aspirants] regarding the abandonment of delusions, realizations, and cessations. Although they speak of differences in realizations, abandonments, and cessations, they explain only one type of practice through which they achieved the resultant state of enlightenment.

It is difficult to hold that with one cause, one can achieve two different results. Although one could say that certain differences could occur due to the length of time spent in the practice of the path, this does not account for the vast differences between the realizations of the Buddha and the *arhats* [those who have gained insight into the true nature of existence, have attained nirvana, and will not be reborn]. As the different path of the Hinayana system alone cannot explain the vast differences between the enlightenment achieved by the Buddha and that achieved by the arhats, it shows that there is another technique that is superior to the Hinayana path.

In any case, according to the explanations of both the Mahayana and Hinayana systems, Buddha Shakyamuni turned the Wheel of Dharma for the first time with his teaching of the Four Noble Truths, and, therefore, an explanation of the Buddha's teachings has to be given on the basis of the Four Noble Truths.

In Buddhism, even as nirvana (the cessation of all suffering) is the ultimate stage, few reach that far. But millions experience samsara *(the indefinitely repeated cycles of birth, misery, and death caused by karma) as "householders"—that is, laypeople—and live a life where some things are under control but most are not: the root of the modern mind's turbulence. What is your advice for the common householder?*

HH: Knowledge or some kind of understanding, a realization about the nature of samsara, the nature of human life, is of great help. When we face our own problems or the problems of others, we begin to understand that those problems are due to the basic nature of samsara. When ordinary things happen, we see them as natural. When something unusual happens, the mind gets upset more easily. If we consider these problems as natural, there is less immediate resentment. At the same time, we are aiming for nirvana because these problems exist. We know, however, that the achievement of nirvana is not easy, and with this in mind, our problems appear smaller.

Every human action, whether good or bad, is based on motivation. Sometimes an action appears rough and negative, but the motivation is pure, sincere, and open. Sometimes we face circumstances that make us angry or frustrated. Once we have gained some understanding of samsara, we can control or at least minimize negative thought in similar circumstances. As a result, our minds will not lose their peace. If we have proper understanding of the path, it will serve as the background to help us face day-to-day difficulties.

Compared to a monk, a householder has more work. You have to look after your husband or wife, your children; and when you have grandchildren, you have even more people to look after. Through this, make a connection with something big—here motivation is most important. In actual life, you sometimes have to speak some harsh words or take strong action in order to protect or benefit the family—here the key point is motivation. The same action, or even tougher action, accomplished with a sincere and good motivation is sincere and good.

For example, an enemy is going to hurt or kill two people. Both take the same counteraction to protect themselves. But one of them does so with a selfish motivation, feeling a strong hatred for the enemy. The other person commits the same counteraction but with a different motivation: *If I allow this person to kill me or do whatever he wants to do, he will harm me, but the ultimate result is that he will sin and he will suffer. Temporarily, he may feel satisfied, but ultimately he will suffer, won't he?* If he takes counteraction in order to save the enemy from wrongdoing, the same action is very different since it arises from a completely different motivation.

For example, when the Chinese invaded Tibet, we were trying to fight them. The motivation was that we sincerely respect the Chinese as human beings who are just like us, who want happiness and no suffering, but we also have to take certain actions to protect ourselves in order to stop the Chinese from wrongdoing, without losing respect and compassion in our thought.

Sometimes Buddhists, even those like myself who are practicing to become bodhisattvas, are negligent about the practice of helping or serving others. The scriptures clearly mention giving one's own body, one's own organs; therefore, engaging in service to society should be the top priority.

How easy or difficult is it for an aspirant to achieve nirvana, in your opinion?

HH: First, you acquire knowledge of the nature of samsara and the nature of nirvana—and the possibility and methods to achieve nirvana, although difficult to implement at the present time. Take my own case. In my situation, it is difficult to carry out certain practices such as samatha. For the practice of samatha, we need to live in complete isolation, in a remote place, for at least a few years, otherwise it is impossible to achieve *samadhi* [a state of one-pointed concentration].

Under the present circumstances, it is impossible for the Dalai Lama to practice like that. Without that quality, there is no possibility to achieve enlightenment in this life—especially *Anuttarayogatantra*, which we practice before the physical body starts to degenerate. Between the ages of 30 and 35, physical energy starts to go down. The age of the present Dalai Lama is 73 years, so from that point of view it is now almost impossible to achieve.

Please give us a hands-on practice for something that afflicts us all uniformly: unfavorable circumstances.

HH: While facing unfavorable circumstances, first of all, keep calm. There is no use feeling anxious or making oneself nervous. The theory of karma and the realization that the entire worldly existence is in the nature of suffering will help maintain calm. Even with the best power of judgment, we may face problems. The most important thing is to keep calm, because only then can we employ the quality of investigation without emotion or anxiety.

Judge calmly and then make a decision. Should that decision prove wrong, have no regrets. That type of attitude is of some help, since we have no clairvoyance. . . .

CHAPTER 3

THE ROLE
OF THE GURU

Why is the "guru" so central to both Buddhist and Hindu traditions?

HH: A guru is the individual who leads you from darkness to light.

Is it a purely religious concept?

HH: The guru as a teacher, philosopher, and guide was a highly revered person in ancient India. Traditionally, the Hindus, the Jains, and the Buddhists attached a lot of importance to a guru. In fact, the position of guru is very important across religions.

The Tibetan equivalent of the guru is a "lama," but is there a difference between them? Does a lama have special qualifications?

HH: The connotation of the words *guru* and *lama* is heaviness—heavy with learning, knowledge, qualification, and kindness. The qualification of a guru primarily refers to his knowledge and kindness. Based on these twin qualifications, you (the disciples) develop admiration, compassion, respect, faith, closeness, and devotion toward your guru. At an individual level, you develop the twin qualities of faith and veneration, and a feeling of closeness.

Often, the word *lama* is mistaken for "living Buddha." But the connotation is very different. Basically, the concept is that one should respect the guru.

In Buddhism, how central is the role of the guru, and what do you see as his or her relevance in the modern world?

HH: The role of a spiritual teacher or master is very important among the followers of Buddhism. The flow of the Buddha's Four Noble Truths is closely tuned in to the law of nature, which prescribes a cause-effect relationship. Just as in the external world there is a cause-effect relationship, within the internal mind, too, there exists this cause-effect relationship.

Now, both altruism and wisdom are qualities of a strong and compassionate mind. From the Buddhist point of view, these fall under the purview of the law of causality. Buddhists believe that everything has a cause. No dramatic change or makeover of the mind takes place without causes and conditions. The law of causality determines each thought and process. One causal condition leads to another and many more thereafter. Therefore, just as altruism (regard for others) has its own causes and conditions, there exist causes and conditions to develop wisdom.

Intrinsic altruism, the innate tendency to respect others as a principle of action and wisdom, brings its own causes and conditions. These factors may be internal or external. The external factor is the presence of a spiritual master or guide, and the internal factor is the knowledge an individual has obtained in this precious life. Training the mind, practicing meditation, will bring forth these qualities of altruism and wisdom.

Wisdom is not confined to any particular type. There are many varieties of wisdom. Realizing and understanding the concept of impermanence, that everything in this world is but momentary and will keep changing with time, is just one kind of wisdom. The concept of impermanence can be detected even by using external scientific instruments. But merely seeing will not carry much conviction. For deeper understanding, an individual will have to see change as a factor and understand it as a nature of reality. That will develop conviction and a deeper understanding of the impermanence. That is wisdom; it is about understanding the absence of independent existence, known as *shunya*. That is where the role of the spiritual teacher or guru is critical.

What is the learning process that enables an individual to become a spiritual master?

HH: Initially, there is only knowledge. With time and constant effort, that knowledge gains depth; and with some more effort, an individual gets an actual experience of his developing wisdom.

In Buddhism, these are termed as wisdom gained through hearing, contemplating, or deep thinking, and from meditation. These are the actual causes—what are known as the substantial causes for developing such wisdom.

There exist two basic types of conditions: the external condition is the teacher, and the internal condition is the healthy body—precious human life. When both these conditions cooperate, a person needs to cultivate the actual cause for the development of wisdom. This clearly shows how the cause-effect relationship works.

The point that I am trying to make here is that the teacher imparts knowledge to his students, but he cannot replace the student. He is just the facilitator; all the hard work and effort has to be put in by the student.

Similarly, Buddhists consider the Buddha as the teacher, the one who will guide and show the right path to his followers and disciples. Those guidelines are based on his own past experiences. Buddhists believe that, initially, the Buddha was just an ordinary human being like the rest of us. But with the help of his teacher, he toiled hard for eons and eons and only then became the Buddha. So, he attained something like a final degree to become a teacher of the highest level, teaching the rest of us how to train our minds.

If the guru is the light that illuminates our path, could you clarify for us the qualities and qualifications of a teacher in Buddhism?

HH: The prime responsibility of a teacher is to teach, to show the right path. When a student goes astray, the teacher should be able to correct the student's mistake so that he doesn't continue on the wrong path. A teacher must possess both knowledge and experience. If he possessed mere intellectual knowledge, he would be unable to correct the mistakes committed by the student.

The necessary qualifications of a teacher have been mentioned extensively in Buddhist texts and scriptures. Different qualifications are prescribed in the scriptures depending on what kind of teacher one is or the field in which the teacher is guiding the student. For example, the qualifications needed for a master of monastic discipline, or *vinaya,* are different from the qualifications necessary for a teacher of bodhisattvas or a teacher of tantra.

The necessary qualifications of a teacher as well as a student are clearly delineated in Aryadeva's Four Hundred Verses, the Catuhsataka. In this text, Aryadeva explains how the teacher should have a deep understanding of the interest and mental capacity of his students. Aryadeva also explains that a teacher must be mentally disciplined. In fact, this is one of the most important qualifications of a teacher. Unless a teacher has disciplined or tamed his own mind, he will be unable to train the mind of his students. For example, vinaya specifies different types of *acharyas,* or teachers, different types of abbots of the monastery, who are required to have certain qualifications, and how if a student is with a resident teacher, he needs to fulfill certain qualifications.

Likewise, in the Bodhisattva Pitaka practice, six perfections are taught to those aspiring to be teachers. Unless they are thoroughly acquainted with the six perfections, they will not be able to preach to others.

Maitreya prescribes ten perfections in Sutralankara. The first and foremost qualification is discipline. The mind of the teacher should be totally disciplined. The process of disciplining the mind should also be in accordance with the major texts and scriptures. Minor realizations, or achievements, which come about by reading a few texts, are simply not enough.

Of the ten qualifications prescribed, the first is the practice and presence of the three precepts—*shila, samadhi,* and *prajna:*

- **Shila**, the first of these three precepts, deals with the presence of ethical discipline or morality. For example, it could be the discipline of a layperson, a monk, or the vows of a bodhisattva or a tantric.

- The second precept deals with the training in one-point meditation, or **samadhi.**

- The third precept, **prajna**, deals with "wisdom realizing emptiness."

In addition to the presence of these three precepts, a teacher must have more qualifications. In terms of learnedness and knowledge, he must be ahead of his students and have more expertise than they do, for he is the one who is sharing his knowledge and guiding them. Furthermore, a teacher must have in-depth knowledge of the subtle connotation of *shunyata,* or emptiness. Then, too, a teacher's qualification is incomplete unless he has compassion for his students. And, last but not least, he should be skilled in explaining the subject that he is teaching and have endless energy and patience to explain it to his students.

Can any individual, from any walk of life or status, become a student?

HH: The important qualifications of a student are explained in detail in Aryadeva's Four Hundred Verses, which states that every student should fulfill three qualifications:

1. He should be unbiased and impartial. If he is biased or partial, he would not be able to keep his objectivity.

2. He should be intelligent enough to differentiate between right and wrong. Also, he should be able to make use of his intelligent mind. For example, if the teacher misguides him, he should be able to pick that up easily and not keep nodding his head and saying yes. If the spiritual master is following a wrong path, which is contrary to mainline teachings, the student should be able to take a stand and not blindly follow that path.

3. Finally, the disciple must be an aspirant, one who relentlessly makes an effort to reinvent his self.

Before a student decides to accept someone as his teacher, he must investigate and know about the person thoroughly. He can do that by attending his discourses and hearing him teach others. This is crucial because a student needs to respect his teacher and look up to him, just like a teacher should have compassion for and show responsibility toward his student. A teacher and a student share a very special bond. Once the student is confident that his teacher has all the qualifications of a good teacher, he can go ahead and form a teacher-student relationship.

The relationship between the teacher and the student should resemble that of a father and son. While the student should possess a feeling of closeness to—and veneration, respect, and regard for—his teacher, a guru should possess a strong sense of responsibility for the well-being of his student.

How does the process of learning begin?

HH: Buddha, the supreme teacher, has taught different lessons to different students, according to their mental disposition. Therefore, one cannot accept his teachings word for word; otherwise many contradictions will open up. In such a situation, an individual will have to judge for himself, understand his words from all angles, and accept them as the true and definitive Buddhist teaching.

A student must learn to categorize the Buddha's levels of teaching as interpretative levels of teaching. For example, if some contradictions are found through analytical meditation in the Buddha's own words, they should not be accepted literally. Even if the Buddha taught it, recognize that it was his way of putting it across to his disciples who had different mental dispositions. He probably taught in such a way purposely.

In Buddhist study, a clear, distinctive line has to be drawn as to whether it is the teaching of the master or the teaching of the text. In fact, the Buddha himself has given this right to his followers to question his own teachings. He said that all the wise men, or *bhikshus*, should accept his teaching only after judging it, and not merely out of respect.

However, by merely listening to the dharma discourse of a teacher, you do not necessarily have to accept him as your guru. For instance, even in the daily process of monastic studies in the Tibetan courtyard, students sit with their learned classmates and discuss various matters; through discussion and debate, they learn a lot of things from each other. That doesn't mean that they have to regard their classmates as their spiritual gurus.

I was wondering . . . if a qualified teacher and an eligible student connect with each other in this life, what happens if one of them passes away? Will they still be able to connect with each other?

HH: If a student relates to his teacher properly in this life, in the course of time such a person will meet a teacher who is equally qualified. Such cases become very clear if you read some of the Buddha's birth stories or the stories of great masters.

Usually a person's search for a guru, a spiritual path, or even God begins with the onset of some acute trauma or emotional disturbance in his or her life. Please comment.

HH: I think that when we feel emotionally or psychologically helpless, we think of praying to a higher power. Buddhists start praying to the Buddha. Whether this is actually beneficial or not is debatable, but from the mental and emotional angle, one benefits and certainly gets some solace and relief.

Different philosophies offer different explanations for why people believe in God. I believe people get some kind of inspiration when they pray and believe in some supreme power. And sometimes they benefit from it. But in faiths like Jainism, as well as Buddhism, everything is according to the law of causality, karma, and past wrongdoings, so there is not much you can do to avoid that.

How, then, does one become a strong individual from within?

HH: In the economic field, we term it self-reliance. In the spiritual field, too, self-reliance is very important.

For instance, if you are strong physically, the body can resist any illness. But if your entire immune system is weak, even the slightest external disturbance can cause a lot of trouble. Similarly, in the world of emotions, if your basic thinking and concepts are strong and there is a tragedy in your life, it may disturb you at a certain emotional level, making you feel unhappy and frustrated. However, the disturbances will pass easily because of your basic mental attitude, your spiritual and inner strength.

There are waves that come and go in the ocean, sometimes tumbling quite powerfully. Underneath, however, the ocean floor remains calm and undisturbed.

With the help of knowledge, awareness, and experience, your mind will remain calm and strong. It depends upon your basic attitude, which has to be strong. Your attitude toward self and others has to be right; then you tend to let the wrong and harmful attitudes go easily, since you have a lot of compassion within you.

Similarly, when something good happens to you, you accept that, too. But since you have a more holistic view, you understand that this is not the one and only event, that there are other events, too, and some of them are not so good. I feel that it is not through religion or faith that you gain better knowledge, but through awareness, which helps you become strong within.

Things are relative. Every event doesn't have just a single cause or condition, but innumerable causes and conditions. So, when something bad happens, you can't blame it on just one factor. Everything is interdependent.

I am very curious about the notion of miracles—for instance, how a guru and a student find each other when the time is right. Do you believe in a realm that goes beyond logic?

HH: According to Buddhist concepts, there are three types of logic. There are three levels of objects of knowledge, three levels of reality. The first one is the obvious: the one that is manifest to us. There is no need to reason. The second reality is known as the slightly hidden, not-so-obvious one; therefore, we have to rely on investigation. The third one is a completely hidden phenomenon.

For example, is there a dog here in front of me or not? The answer is obvious since there is no dog that can be seen here. Simple.

Now, is there a dog that you can't see behind the chair or not? You might think that since the chair was prepared for the Dalai Lama, and since no dog has been seen running about after his arrival, there is no dog there.

With regard to the third level of reality, known as the completely hidden phenomenon, let us take the example of my own date of birth: July 6, 1935. There's no way to know that fact by myself. I cannot investigate it and can only rely upon a third person—my mother or someone. I know that there is no reason for my mother to lie. This is the point that I was trying to make—that a person should know when to rely on a third person's word.

So, there are various levels of reality. I feel that when we say "logic," we mean something closer to common sense. Suppose someone is concentrating deeply or is in a deep samadhi, and the subtle energy becomes more active, and some objects start moving. According to the first level of reality, one would consider the moving objects to be a miracle. But if you think beyond that level and know how the system works, it will not be a miracle in your eyes. According to the law of causality, the internal element acts upon the external element in such a way that things may move or change.

CHAPTER 4

COMPASSION
AND HAPPINESS

You frequently use the words <u>love</u> and <u>compassion.</u> What is the difference between them?

HH: I do not know the exact difference between *love* and *compassion*. In Sanskrit, there is the word *karuna;* and in Tibetan, there are two words, *inji* and *chamba*. *Chamba* means a desire to have happiness, whereas *karuna* and *inji* mean the desire to overcome suffering.

Genuine compassion does not depend upon whether the other is nice to me; it is based on the realization and acceptance that the other is also a central being and has the right to be happy and overcome suffering, irrespective of his or her attitude to me. Even an enemy who is harming me is a central being and has every right to overcome suffering, to achieve happiness.

So, genuine compassion is a sense of concern for everyone. Compassion is not pity; it is based on respect for the other's rights and a recognition that the other is just like myself.

Compassion is, then, virtuous and desirable, but how does compassion make me a happier or better human being?

HH: I will answer this with an example. When I meet someone on the street, I am reassured of my human feelings. Regardless of whether I know him or not, I smile at him. Sometimes there is no response; sometimes there is suspicion. But I get the benefit of smiling. Whether the other person gets any benefit or not depends upon his own thinking as well as on the circumstances.

The rewards of practicing compassion go first to the practitioner. I believe it is very important to understand this; otherwise, we will believe that compassion benefits the other and has nothing for us.

A compassionate attitude helps you communicate easily with fellow human beings and other central beings. As a result, you make more genuine friends; the atmosphere is more positive, which gives you inner strength. This inner strength helps you voluntarily concern yourself with others, instead of just thinking about your own self.

Scientific research has shown that those individuals who often use words such as *me, I,* and *mine* face a greater risk of a heart attack. If one always thinks of oneself, one's thinking becomes very narrow; even a small problem appears very significant and unbearable.

When we think of others, our minds widen, and within that large space, even big personal problems may appear insignificant. This, according to me, makes all the difference.

Your Holiness, you have carried the burden of the suffering of your people and your homeland for so many years. Yet you carry a lightness of being, a spontaneous joy, that touches all whom you meet. How do you do this?

HH: Nothing special! Good sleep, good food! I don't think it is one particular thing, but it is the attitude toward oneself, toward others. Life is not easy from the Buddhist point of view. This body is a hindrance; negative karma or samsaric karma can create problems. You also sometimes see unfortunate things happen. But unfortunate things can be transformed into a positive event; you can use them to gain experience. Therefore, they are helpful in daily life.

Of course, one must avoid negative consequences from the beginning. But once something happens, try to look at it from different perspectives. For example, we have lost our country. This situation, however, also presents new opportunities; if you look at it from a positive aspect, the frustrations become less.

What is this change of attitude that makes a person feel happy?

HH: As a Buddhist monk, my main aim is to practice altruism, the practice of bodhicitta, with wisdom or awareness. I believe that analytical meditation is one of the key methods to transform the mind and the emotions. This has brought me inner peace and strength. Such a method also allows one to change perceptions and attitudes toward oneself, others, and immediate problems.

I feel that the foremost change would be that as one develops a sense of concern, of compassion for others, one's mind broadens or widens. At that point, an individual's problems and suffering appear very small.

How do we develop concern for others and for ourselves?

HH: One could start by analyzing the value of negative feelings, or ill feelings, toward others. Consider what that means to you, and how you feel about yourself. Next, probe the value of such a mental attitude and the value of a mind that shows concern and compassion for others.

I am suggesting you analyze and make comparisons between these two mental attitudes. From my experience, I have found that insecurity and a lack of self-confidence brings about fears, frustrations, and depression. However, if your nature changes to a selfless concern for the welfare of others, you will experience calmness, a sense of inner strength, and self-confidence.

The capacity for compassion that one has for others is the measuring rod for one's own mental state, and compassion develops an inner strength. It is unnecessary to see the results of our acts of compassion. In some cases, our sense of compassion may not be appreciated. Many people have the impression that the practice of love, compassion, and forgiveness is of benefit to others, but will serve no specific purpose to one's own self. I think that is wrong. These positive emotions will immediately help one's own mental state.

The Buddhists have a fascinating attitude toward what is called the "enemy." For instance, some monks pray on mats that have the message PRAY FOR THE CHINESE *on them. What benefit does it bring them?*

HH: For genuine Buddhist practitioners, the enemy of the community presents a real opportunity to practice patience and tolerance. In order to improve genuine compassion, the practice of tolerance is essential. For the practice, the enemy is very important. That's one way to look at it.

In the Mahayana school of Buddhism, we refer to other beings as mother-centered beings. There is no point in excluding those people who create trouble. In our case, our Chinese brothers and sisters are also mother-centered beings; hence, we have to consider them.

There is one good example of a monk who spent more than 17 years in a Chinese prison, or labor camp. He had been with me before 1959. In the late 1980s, he joined me in Dharamsala. Because we know each other very well, I asked him about his experiences. He said that on a few occasions he faced real danger. I assumed that he meant danger to his life. "What danger?" I asked. "The danger of losing compassion for the Chinese" was his answer.

I think this is a very wonderful thing to say. I think that is the reflection of the practice. Not all Tibetans share this view.

One day I asked a Tibetan from my own village whether he felt angry with the Chinese. Before his answer or words came, his cheeks began to shake and his face became red. He said, "Of course, yes." So, such people are also there. There are all kinds of people.

41

Your Holiness, could you share with us your personal practice of bodhicitta in daily life?

HH: For more than 35 years, I have been reciting the Eight Verses of Thought Transformation every day. I had received an oral transmission and teachings on the verses from Trijang Rinpoche. Although I cannot spend much time on them, I usually recite and think a little about them. This is something very useful. The composer of this text is Kadampa Master Geshe Langri Thangpa.

The great master of Dharma saw the practice of bodhicitta, exchanging self with others, as the most important part of his practice. I shall explain these verses briefly.

1. With the determination to accomplish the highest welfare of all sentient beings, who excel even the wish-granting jewel, may I at all times hold them dear.

The kindness of sentient beings toward us is not merely confined to the achievement of our final goal: enlightenment. The fulfillment of our temporary aims, such as the experience of happiness and so on, also depends on their kindness. Therefore, sentient beings are superior even to the wish-fulfilling jewel. We say the prayer *May I be able to hold them dearer than the wish-fulfilling jewel.*

2. Whenever I associate with others, may I think myself the lowest of all and from the depth of my heart hold the others supreme.

When we meet others, we should not think of ourselves as superior and look down on them or pity them, but see them as the source of our happiness. We should hold them dear and revere them because they have the equal capacity of the activities of the Buddha, like granting us happiness and enlightenment.

3. In all actions, may I search my mind, and as soon as delusions arise, endangering myself and others, may I firmly face and avert them.

When we engage in such noble practices, we might encounter obstacles. These are not external but internal. They come from our own minds; they are delusions of our own minds. The real enemy is within us, not outside. When we are able to discipline and control the mind through training and effort, we will gain real peace and tranquility. When the mind is out of control, we lose our inner peace, our happiness, immediately.

Ultimately, the constructive power is within us, as is the destructive power. So it rests in our own hands. The Buddha said, therefore, you are your own master, and everything depends on your mind-set.

In the practice of bodhicitta, we have to refrain from all types of nonvirtues. Primarily, we must avoid anger. Anger can never produce happiness, whereas attachment can bring about the experience of happiness, in certain cases. Therefore, for someone who practices bodhicitta, the biggest enemy is anger. We have a saying in Tibet: *if you lose your temper and get angry, bite your knuckles.* This means that if you lose your temper, do not show it to others. Rather, bite your *own* knuckles.

4. When I see beings of wicked nature, pressed
    by violent nonvirtues and afflictions, may I
    hold them dear as if I had found a rare and
    precious treasure.

When many people are excited by emotional afflictions and pressed by delusions, Sravaka and Pratyekabuddhas—practitioners of the Hinayana vehicle—tend
to avoid them because they are afraid of getting involved
and carried away themselves. Bodhisattvas, on the other
hand, face them bravely and take their chance in bring-
ing happiness to other sentient beings.

5. When others out of envy treat me badly with
    slander, abuse, and the like, may I suffer the
    defeat and offer the victory to them.

When other beings, especially some who hold a
grudge against you, abuse and harm you out of envy,
you should not abandon them, but hold them as objects
of the greatest compassion and take care of them. The
practitioner should absorb the loss himself or herself and
offer victory to the others. Practitioners of bodhicitta do
this not with the intention of becoming virtuous, but
rather with the motivation of helping other sentient
beings.

6. When the one whom I have benefited with
    great hope hurts me badly, may I behold him
    as my supreme guru.

When from among those who have a personal
grudge against you, there is someone whom you have

helped and he repays your kindness in a wrong way, you might feel that you do not want to help him ever again. It is very difficult not to hold this against him, and this becomes a great stumbling block for the practitioner of altruism. However, a practitioner should care specially for such a person. A person who harms you must also be seen as someone who is your spiritual guide. You will find that your enemy is your supreme teacher.

7. In short, may I directly and indirectly offer
the benefit and happiness to all my mothers.
May I secretly take upon myself the harmful
actions and sufferings of my mothers.

Everyone wishes to achieve happiness and to avoid suffering. When we remember that others are infinite in number and you yourself are only one, no matter how superior you are, others become more valuable. And if you have some power of judgment, you will find that it is worthwhile to sacrifice yourself for the sake of others. One person must not sacrifice an infinite number of others for the sake of himself.

At this point I usually recommend a special visualization. See yourself as a very selfish person, and in front of you a great number of sentient beings are undergoing suffering. To get an even clearer picture of sentient beings, visualize them actively experiencing their sufferings. You yourself remain as a third person, neutral and unbiased.

Then see which side you want to take. Analyze which one is more worthwhile—the welfare of one person or the welfare of many beings. If they thought like this, even the most selfish politicians would, without hesitation, join the majority. How sad it is to be selfish!

One who practices taking onto himself all the sufferings and faults of all other sentient beings from the depth of his heart also trains in sharing with others all the good qualities such as virtues and happiness that he has in himself.

Train yourself. Initially it is very difficult for your selfish attitude to decrease, and you cannot control it easily. But if you persevere for a long time, you will be successful.

The first seven verses deal with the practice and method of Conventional Bodhicitta, and the eighth verse deals with the practice of Ultimate Bodhicitta wisdom.

8. May all this remain undefiled by the stains
    of the eight worldly principles; may I, by perceiving all dharmas as illusory, unattached
    be delivered from the bondage of cyclic
    existence.

If someone undertakes such a practice motivated by worldly concerns such as wishing for a long and healthy life, happiness, and perfection in this life, it is basically wrong. And if someone practices hoping that people might call him a great religious practitioner and so forth, it is definitely wrong. And if someone practices bodhicitta, altruism, and views all the objects of his compassion or all sentient beings as truly existent, that is also wrong.

You should undertake this practice with the understanding that all phenomena are illusions. One understands that all phenomena are illusions by the force of having refuted or negated their true existence. What is left behind is mere imputation—mere label and designation, which are illusions. Although they appear as though truly existent, they lack true existence.

Your book The Art of Happiness *has been a bestseller in the West. In the East, the pursuit of happiness seems like a very Western concept. How do you look at happiness?*

HH: Happiness, nirvana, or moksha is freedom from suffering, from negative emotion, from the serfdom of ignorance. This is the concept of Dharma, especially in Indian philosophy, where liberation from ignorance—happiness—is the goal. All beings are equal in the sense that all, including animals, have a right to be happy.

People believe that economic difficulties, illiteracy, and ill health lead to unhappiness. They pay a lot of attention to material development. However, even in the developed countries of the West, people are experiencing loneliness, anxiety, and fear deep inside, often due to greed, discontent, and mental unrest. Neither money nor technology can help to develop inner peace, which requires the right kind of mental attitude. The problems are caused by human intelligence, and we must find the answer also within human intelligence.

Today, scientists inform us that increased movements in certain parts of the brain are positive. Soon people will realize that inner tranquility is based on a more open mind and heart, a sense of concern toward all humanity as one entity. With such a concept, to achieve our own happiness we have to respect the rights of others to be happy. This may seem idealistic, but human history has shown us that many things that have looked unrealistic as a blueprint have worked out eventually.

We want happiness, the happiness that comes from within us—inexpensive, isn't it? A happiness and peace that nobody can destroy, steal, or take away. This inner peace is most precious. The basis of inner peace is love and compassion. If you agree, implement it; if you do not agree, that is all right, too.

Even after all these long years of refuge and being so far from home, Tibetans in India generally look so peaceful. Your Holiness always radiates this joy, which is so infectious, so wonderful to see! What is the secret?

HH: Thank you very much. As I said at the beginning, I myself am very happy. In fact, this morning, I felt excited because this is the first time that I have given some lectures or Buddhist explanations to our Indian friends. I feel and always express that if the glories of the Buddha's teachings had not flourished in this country or not reached our homeland, Tibet would still be a dark country. But the light of Buddha's teachings reached Tibet through many difficult roads and difficult periods and remained there for quite a number of centuries.

Today, these teachings give tremendous happiness and satisfaction to thousands of human souls on this side of the long Himalayan range. As a result, many people have the same opinion that Tibetans, including myself, are a happy people, jovial and joyful, I think. This may be to some extent the effect of the environment and the small population, with no worries over food and shelter in this big land. The main factor, however, is the Buddha's teachings—of compassion, kindness, and tolerance.

Whether individual Tibetans know Buddhism well or not does not matter. A certain kind of environment has developed around them because of the teachings. We are grateful for the work of the Indian Masters. I always regard myself as a disciple of this country, a disciple of Indian Masters. Today, Indian Masters have *become* disciples; a disciple has become a teacher. This is some kind of contribution, I feel, some kind of repayment for Indian help and kindness. I really have some kind of special, extraordinary feeling. Thank you very much.

CHAPTER 5

SUFFERING

Your Holiness, suffering is the single greatest affliction that haunts humanity. What is the root of suffering?

HH: There may be many different causes for our suffering, but the prevailing one is attachment and desire. Desire has its root in ignorance. There are many different types of ignorance, but the one we are talking about here is the ignorance that misconceives the nature of reality. No matter how forceful our ignorant mind appears, it has no valid foundation.

The ignorance we are concerned with has two parts: a self-grasping attitude focused by the person on himself and a self-grasping attitude focused on external objects. Within the context of suffering and pleasure, all phenomena are divided into two: the being who suffers and external phenomena. It represents the self-grasping attitude of the individual, who out of ignorance grasps at his own existence as being independent and permanent. This self-grasping focuses on external objects, believing them to also have an independent, inherent existence.

We determine whether something exists or not through the consciousness that realizes it. Both phenomena, the temporary and the permanent, fall into these categories of existent or nonexistent objects. The fact that some phenomena exist occasionally shows that they depend on causes and conditions; and, therefore, they are called products. On the other hand, the phenomena that do not depend on causes and conditions exist permanently or eternally, and they are called nonproducts.

Let us test ourselves: When we recollect happy memories or a very anxious time, we go through such fluctuating states of mind as *I had such great pleasure that time,* or *I had such a hard time,* and so on. At that time, we should reflect, *Who is that "I," that self that I feel so vividly about?* Reflect whether you identify that "I" with your body or with your consciousness.

What do you think? Is it your consciousness or your mind? "I" and "mind"—are they the same? If so, could you say, "my mind"? That seems difficult!

If suffering is such an intrinsic part of our existence, how, then, can we overcome it? You also say that before we embark on the process to end suffering, we must be sure that suffering can be ended; we must have proof. How can we find this proof?

HH: The state in which one is permanently freed from suffering is called nirvana. Everlasting happiness is explained as freedom from suffering, and the means by which one accomplishes such a state is the truth of the path to the cessation of suffering.

What basis has one to free oneself from suffering? We have to free ourselves from suffering through consciousness. The truth of the path to the cessation of suffering is a very refined state of mind, endowed with a special quality of wisdom. Therefore, the wish to rid ourselves of suffering is consciousness or mind, and the method to free ourselves from suffering is also consciousness or mind. We have to free our minds from suffering, and its stains have to be eliminated from the sphere of our reality.

The truth of the path to the cessation of suffering—the consciousness—that eliminates these mental delusions is the one that also realizes this reality, this nature. Therefore, it is important to understand what is meant by the nature of emptiness.

As the cause of suffering can be purged or eliminated, suffering itself can be eliminated. The reason why we can eliminate suffering is because its cause is action, karma, and the inducing factor of motivation, which all stem from the deluded mind. Although the possibility to eliminate karma does exist, one has also to understand karma. Although it is a cause, it has to be reactivated to have a result; basically the root cause is delusion. When we talk about the possibility of eliminating delusion, all these delusions are rooted in the self-grasping attitude. It comes back to the point of how to clarify consciousness, which perceives phenomena as inherently existent.

Although all Buddhist schools talk of methods of eliminating this mistaken consciousness, the superior method is the one explained in the Madhyamika system. By using logical reasoning for the negation of inherent existence, one can understand the nature of emptiness. Through such analyses, one can also establish that the mind can be freed of delusion.

Is there a specific process to lessen suffering?

HH: We all have this innate wish for happiness, and we shun suffering. In addition to these natural desires, we also have the right to achieve happiness and be free of suffering. Buddhists say this is a natural right.

There are many different categories of happiness and suffering, which can broadly be divided into physical pleasure and suffering, and mental happiness and suffering. Of the body and the mind, the mind is the more important factor; and, therefore, the experiences of the mind are more important. Buddha said that the methods by which one can achieve happiness and free oneself from suffering do exist.

The Western view says that the roots of suffering can be biological—the biochemistry of the brain. They can also arise out of childhood experiences; from repressed emotions; and from anxieties, negative feelings, and self-defeating habits. The Western model is not very encouraging because you cannot avoid these afflictions; at best, you can hope for some reflective distance from them.

HH: As you rightly pointed out, feelings can be explained biologically, but to what extent? From the Buddhist viewpoint—and all those schools of thought that accept the continuation of life—one explanation stands out: what we call karmic imprints or dispositions. Even in one lifetime, you experience things in early life that result in various kinds of dispositions and leave certain impressions or imprints on the mind.

According to the usual explanations, every thought results from some change in the brain or nervous system, some chemical reaction. In some cases, the opposite occurs—that is, first the thought comes, and as a result of it, some chemical changes occur in the body. Do you think that is possible or not? If so, how come?

First, it is accepted that consciousness, mind, or thought is a product of brain activity or some physical process. That's the basis. Every experience of the mind must develop on the basis of something happening in the body. That is fundamental. Then how can changes in thought bring about changes in the physical body?

Roughly speaking, sometimes when one's physical condition is not normal, frustration and anger develop easily. But if you are physically healthy, your mood is happier. Sometimes without apparent change, subtle changes may still occur. For instance, when your mood is pleasant and calm, some past memory or even just some fleeting thought may cause physical change.

On the grosser level, certain mental attitudes arise because of physical change. In other cases, something is happening at a purely mental level that causes physical change. If that is the case, how, then, did the mental element develop?

Let's talk about hatred and anger. The Western solution would be to be able to hate and to get over hatred, but not to get over the ability to hate. If you are unable to hate, you are not quite okay; if you can only hate and not get over it, that's also not okay. How does Buddhism approach hatred and aggression?

HH: We have to find effective ways to deal with negative emotions because I feel that people with negative emotions form a majority of the human population. This is the basis of secular ethics, without any belief or religion. I personally also sometimes use these methods—that is, I analyze the usefulness of negative emotions such as hatred. Once you develop a very strong feeling of hatred, it is difficult to say whether this feeling harms the person you hate. The other person may be unaffected, but your hatred affects *you;* and eventually you lose your happiness, appetite, or sleep.

Hatred, therefore, is of no use. Analyze the situation. If the result is that you need some kind of a countermeasure, it is a question of whether it is just or unjust. If the person has done something unjust to you, you have the right to counter it. Look at it the other way. You can bring about some kind of countermeasure without hatred as well. Usually, I see this comes through thinking.

Attachment is more complicated. If you let these negative emotions grow, they are limitless. They lead to trouble, dissatisfaction. It is better to limit negative emotions such as desire, attachment, pride, and the like.

So must we eliminate them completely, or are you suggesting limits?

HH: Oh yes, limits, of course. At the human level, there is no possibility of elimination. For the Buddhist practitioner, once you accept the concept of nirvana or moksha, you accept the possibility of eliminating all these negative emotions.

Take desire. There are different kinds of desire. At the mental level, I think, it is helpful to make distinctions. For example, even with anger, there can be positive and negative anger. Anger, I think, can also come out of concern, out of affection. That kind of anger is certainly positive and leads to positive action.

What about anger in protecting one's rights? Would you say that it is a "positive anger"?

HH: I think that in defending or protecting one's own rights, disregarding the suffering of others is extreme. Others also have their rights, and I also have the right to defend *my* rights, to achieve something on my own. Such feelings are, of course, right.

Desire can be positive or negative—even the feeling of ego or a strong sense of self. In order to develop will and determination, in order to save other people, and in order to do good work, you need self-confidence. For that you need a strong sense of self. "I can do it," "I must not abandon this work"—a strong sense of self is very necessary to say these things.

One may think of oneself as so strong that one has no hesitation in harming others and disregarding their rights. This kind of ego or sense of self is negative. You see two extremes.

But when anger is directed toward a terrorist group that causes death and anguish to hundreds of people, how does one deal with this seemingly "justified" anger?

HH: Under certain circumstances, we need forms of countermeasures. If someone takes advantage of you unreasonably or unlawfully, of course, it is your right to counter it—but do it without anger and without hatred. That we can do, although it is not easy. In reality, a countermeasure taken by analytical meditation rather than hatred is more effective. These are the ways of shaping our mind. As time goes by, the realization about how harmful—how useless and destructive—negative emotions are sets in.

By appreciating a positive mind, your whole attitude toward negative emotions can change. You become cautious about negative emotions. Mentally, some kind of distance develops by itself. Eventually, these negative emotions will lessen and not get inflamed as often as before, while positive emotions will increase in the meantime.

That's the way of changing or transforming our minds. More work on the mind through analytical meditation and single-pointed meditation increases its sharpness and alertness. Finally, the most important result is that as a more compassionate attitude develops, it automatically reduces fear and increases self-confidence, determination, and willpower. Willpower out of pride is also blind, but self-confidence with sincere motivation? That's sound.

Does Buddhism value passion and ecstasy as a positive human state?

HH: I don't know. If we achieve nirvana or moksha, I think it is worthwhile to be excited, but in my experience it is usually better to stay more balanced. Too much excitement may lead to too much unhappiness. Too many ups and down are also not good. Maybe that way of life or thinking is less colorful, but in the long run, even physically it is better. That is my experience or my feeling.

If Lord Buddha says suffering can be eliminated, then into what phenomenon does it transform and cease to be?

HH: Into the nature of emptiness. So, the nature of emptiness into which all suffering has dissolved or purified is also a quality of samsara, cyclic existence. Emptiness as a quality of samsara and of nirvana are identical. When we realize the nature of samsara, we have reached nirvana.

Another explanation is that if consciousness—the mind that sentient beings in samsara have inherent in themselves—is left to the influence of a negative state of mind, such a state is known as samsara. On the other hand, if a person controls her or his own mind and keeps it in its intrinsic nature, that is nirvana. This is very difficult.

If we find ourselves very disturbed by a negative state of mind, the negative state should first be turned into a neutral state and later transformed into a virtuous state. As long as we feel anger, it is almost impossible to switch to compassion or some other positive feeling. First, try to transform that negative mind into a neutral one.

Samsara is cyclic existence; one rotates in the cycle of existence. One can also gain some understanding from the fact that nirvana, because it is cessation, is regarded as a permanent phenomenon and samsara—cyclic existence—is an impermanent phenomenon.

The sage Nagarjuna said that complete understanding of samsara is nirvana. Nirvana is a state completely free from suffering. It is a cessation of suffering.

CHAPTER 6

MOTIVATION ON
THE SPIRITUAL PATH

Your Holiness, motivation is a key aspect of spiritual evolution in Buddhist philosophy . . .

HH: Motivation is most important, and a saying goes: *If one makes an effort, liberation can be achieved even while remaining with the family.* On the other hand, if one has no initiative, even abandoning family life to live in isolation will not achieve liberation. This is very true.

If the central motivation for all human activities is compassion, then all activities become humanized. Without compassion, our activities become too mechanical. If our activity in every field—education, economy, technology, scientific research—is motivated by sincere compassion, and not just by how much profit is possible or by temporary benefits, it will benefit others. Our daily activities then become the actions of a bodhisattva.

However, there is a distinction in philosophy between motivation and method. For example, Gandhi distinguished between the method and the goal, the means and the end. How do you draw this distinction?

HH: Ultimately, it is based upon motivation. Take, for example, violence and nonviolence. If sincere compassion is the motivation, a harsh word or action, such as that of parents to children or a teacher to a student, cannot be called violence. Even if it appears outwardly harsh, it is ultimately nonviolent. In the same way, if there is negative emotion or negative motivation—for example, if one wants to cheat another or to take advantage of another, and yet uses kind words, it is actually a kind of violence. So motivation is the most important factor. Having said that, if the method used is drastically violent, it cannot be justified by saying the motivation is right.

Your Holiness, for Buddhists their motivation is preeminent, and for Hindus the method is important. Could you elaborate on that?

HH: These two factors are equally important. In order to have good motivation, there must be a good aim to which one aspires.

Once, when we were discussing violence and nonviolence, I think it was India's late prime minister Morarji Desai who told me that method is very important. In the Buddhist view, motivation and result are more important than the means. Despite good motivation, good results, violence is always bad; and some people believe that.

In the Buddhist view, if motivation is good, the result is good.

In Tibet, there was a statue of the Buddha in the open. It was raining. A person passing by saw the statue and thought, *How can rain fall on the statue, on the body of the Buddha?* So he looked around for something to cover it with. He could find nothing other than the soles of old shoes, so he covered the statue with the soles.

Another person passed by and thought, *How can anyone place old soles on the statue of the Buddha?* So he took them away. Since the motivation was good in both cases, there was no harm done.

Would you say that even on the spiritual path, there are different types of motivation? For instance, compassion and bodhicitta are considered the greatest motivations to seek Buddhahood.

HH: The best type of motivation is bodhicitta—that is, to achieve enlightenment for the sake of other sentient beings. The next best is that we should at least aspire to achieve liberation. The third type of motivation is that we should be free from attachment to the affairs of this lifetime and should aim for happiness in all future lives.

First of all, in order to cultivate appropriate or correct motivation, reflect that this life that we hold so dear passes so quickly. If it were something durable, something eternal, it would be worth holding dear. A lifetime is limited to a maximum of 100 years—in some rare cases, to 120 or 130 years. Beyond that it is impossible for an ordinary human being to live. So always remember impermanence.

When the phenomenon called death occurs, things like wealth, fame, power, and so on accumulated in this lifetime cannot help us. Life itself is a phenomenon that changes momentarily. If someone totally neglects to provide for future lives and is too preoccupied with the concerns of this life alone, and in his eagerness to have a good time in this life, he grasps too much or has too great an attachment to this life, he will face many more problems in the end.

From the beginning, our attitude should be well balanced toward this life. *Yes, these are the facts; this is reality*—a feeling that this is okay, a somewhat relaxed attitude. . . . Then, when things become difficult, the depth of mental disturbance will be less. Sometimes it is very helpful to read the biographies of those people who have more experience of life. We should contemplate the fact that when people are too preoccupied with the affairs of this life, they face more adverse circumstances, whereas when people adopt a rational and more realistic approach to life, they have less trouble and difficulties.

If bodhicitta is the supreme motivation, how does one generate it?

HH: To generate bodhicitta, we reflect on the fact that just like ourselves, all sentient beings, equally, have the natural tendency to desire happiness and avoid suffering; and everyone, equally, has a right to get rid of suffering and to achieve happiness. The only difference is that you are one single person, whereas the others are limitless, infinite in number. In other words, you are in the minority, and the others are the majority. Although there is a big difference in number, it is the same feeling: *I want happiness; they want happiness. I do not want suffering; they do not want suffering.*

So there is a clear relation between us and others. We depend on others. Without others, we cannot gain any happiness—not in the past, not today, and not in the future.

If we think more about the welfare of others, we ourselves will ultimately reap the benefit. While thinking along these lines, we will find that others are more important than ourselves, and we will come to the conclusion that our own fate is a question of one person. If one has to undergo suffering in order to bring about happiness for the infinite number of others, it is really worthwhile to suffer. On the other hand, if in order to achieve happiness just for one person, many others have to suffer, that is very wrong.

Eventually, think more about *shunyata*, emptiness. That is the starting point to take up the offensive with your inner enemy. Ultimately it is your own motivation.

Your Holiness, if motivation determines the meaning of an act rather than its consequences or the action itself, how does one practice correct motivation, especially when we know that until one achieves enlightenment, the mind is in various stages of delusion?

HH: Do you mean that Buddhists talk about the importance of good motivation, but until we reach enlightenment, our minds are deluded, so how can one have good motivation?

As I mentioned before, in order to fight with the inner enemy, the first Buddhist step is on the defensive level, the second on the offensive level. In the first phase, we are not in a position to defeat delusions. We employ defensive tactics so as not to fall under the influence of more delusions. The immediate practice one can engage in is to restrain one's physical and verbal actions from nonvirtues—the ten nonvirtuous actions, including killing, stealing, and sexual misconduct for laymen. This is the immediate practice.

Everybody regards killing as something bad. The law sometimes even gives a death sentence. Everybody agrees that stealing is bad. If there are a few policemen watching, one refrains from killing and stealing, posing as a good citizen. But if there is nobody watching, one acts differently, and that is wrong. A practitioner of the Buddha Dharma should always be able to observe pure morality on his own, whether there is a policeman there or not. A practitioner has his own police force within himself; he is always alert.

Always examine whether your motivation is pure or not; always check yourself. As soon as you wake up in the morning, start the day with something like a mental master plan. Decide, till death—and particularly this month, this day—*I shall lead a life of moral principles and not engage in anything that brings harm to others, even if I cannot help them.* That is the kind of master plan early in the morning. If you are in business, engineering, educational work, or any other field, observe high moral principles. This is important even in warfare.

If you have to deal with killing, do it with high principles and in the context of human life. Do not lose human feeling. Kill only when absolutely necessary. In modern warfare, there is less and less of human feeling because everything is mechanized. Machines have no mercy, no human feeling, so naturally wars become very destructive. Women and children are killed . . . there is no way to avoid this. A bomb has no conscience, no discrimination to kill or not to kill, so everybody will be killed.

We place too much emphasis on machines. We should lead our daily lives with some principles. Just like the police force, the intelligence force must be here inside ourselves, and our supreme court must also be within us. Whether there is a supreme court or not, as a judge, a policeman, a punisher, punish yourself if you do something wrong, not necessarily physically, but even mentally—regret it; confess.

Later, before you go to sleep, just as someone involved in making money will calculate his profit every night, similarly make some calculation of mental activities experienced during the day. How many negative activities and how many positive mental activities happened? And because we are giving it special attention, our behavior will improve as time goes by. In the beginning, even a person who is easily irritable will become gentler.

According to my own experience, behavior can be improved. This is the first level of practice. Once you gain some kind of inner strength and self-discipline to control such misdeeds and become a good, honest, warmhearted person—not harming others—there is more compassion, more love, and more kindness. As these qualities increase, you become more stable, more courageous, and your willpower increases. These are good human qualities, aren't they?

In addition, drink less alcohol if it is not possible to give it up. Cigarettes are also very harmful to your health and your teeth. You have very beautiful white teeth, and to make them dirty is silly, isn't it? We want a healthy body, but we smoke and drink—that is a contradiction.

You need not be a monk or *brahmachari* [monastic student], but you can lead the life of one—very pure, very sincere.

Compassion and warmheartedness are what we can call universal religion, whether we believe in reincarnation or not, whether we believe in God or not. For Buddhists, it does not matter whether we believe in the Buddha or not. It is most important to be a good human being. Sooner or later we have to die, and then if we review and regret all the past years, it is too late.

Spend each day of your life in a good and useful way; at least do not harm others, if you cannot help them. When the final day comes, you will be very happy, very satisfied. Some of your friends may cry, but you yourself will feel happy, won't you? There will be no regrets. As a Buddhist, you cultivate good seeds in this lifetime, and although there is nobody who gives you a guarantee, you already have the guarantee that your next life will be a better one.

CHAPTER 7

KARMA

Your Holiness, I would like to start the dialogue on karma by asking you what brings me here. It started with my visiting you officially in the late '60s, and I find myself back again, and I have no conscious volition other than a kind of urge that brings me here—an urge I do not feel I have much control over. Is this my karma, and is free will an illusion, then?

HH: We have no control over actions of karma that we have accumulated in the past. We have to experience their results. But we do have control over our own karma insofar as what we experience in the future, which is determined by our own actions at the present time.

All our experiences are consequences of our own past karma, our actions. There are certain differences in a relative way, for instance, when we talk of death. There are three types of death: as a consequence of karma, when one's merit is exhausted, and accidental death. However, all of these are interrelated and, broadly speaking, are due to one's own karma, to one's own past—for within them is also the issue of what is the cause of one's death in each particular case. In the same way, there is illness due to karma, due to an imbalance of humors, imbalances in the body, the influence of spirits, and the like.

Here, the explanation of two factors—causes and circumstances—becomes necessary. Conditions refer to immediate circumstances. This is said to be something that one can manipulate, gain control over.

There is no control over karma that we have accumulated in the past. Those actions have been done, and only imprints are left on our consciousness. We have to experience their results. What we are going to experience in the future is in our own hands and is determined by us. For example, if we have committed a crime, we have to face the consequences of that action, unless we have the possibility of taking some purifying measures.

There is a kind of back door; there is a possibility of neutralizing karma through practices of confession and purification. In the same way, good karma accumulated in the past can be destroyed through forceful, non-virtuous actions such as anger. It is also possible that one forceful action, karma, overwhelms another action.

If every individual carries his personal karma into the next life, how do we explain the increase in the world population? There must be a finite number of individuals who carry forward their karma into future lives. Even if we accept the idea that many of them will be in karmic transition as other forms of sentient beings, the total number of sentient beings also seems to be growing—look at the mosquito population in

Dharamsala. Where are all these beings and creatures coming from?

HH: Many systems of the universe are infinite; therefore, sentient beings are infinite in number. Whole universes disappear at one stage. At the same time there are infinite galaxies; some are forming, some remaining, others disappearing. After destruction, a particular place remains empty—just space. Then again, new galaxies form. It is infinite—we are like tourists: we come, remain some time, and go without expenses.

Why does this infinite journey of consciousness spin into a duality of perfection and imperfection—into karma? Why this split between illusion and reality, and how does one overcome it?

HH: Aryadeva in his Four Hundred Verses says that all substantial matter, even atomic particles, has beginningless continuity—no beginning. That means that if we were to look for the continuity of the materials of this book, we would seek further for its cause, its substantial cause, its indirect cause, and so on. In the end, we would find that there is no beginning at all. But if we burned this book, then there is an end to it, to the phenomenon we label "this book."

When we go to Buddhahood, the basic consciousness has no beginning and no end; however, certain consciousnesses such as ignorance, hatred, anger, and attachment—the negative thoughts—have no beginning, but they have an end. This book has an end because there is a possibility of a factor that is the antidote to its

71

continuity by which it can be destroyed. In the same way, these negative aspects of the consciousness have their opposite factors, which serve as antidotes for removing them.

The same applies to our self-grasping attitude. Because it is mistaken and distorted, it is mistaken consciousness and, therefore, lacks valid support. On the other hand, wisdom, which realizes emptiness—which is the opposite factor of that mistaken consciousness—has valid support because it is valid cognition. Because these two consciousnesses directly contradict each other in their ways of engaging in the object, one is the antidote of the other. And the self has to bring about that resolution.

Ultimately there has to be a resolution when we reach Buddhahood or nirvana—the opposition has to be resolved. Since there is that contradiction, and since one of the two factors has valid support and the other lacks it, the one that lacks valid support is later overcome and eliminated. One has also to understand that the nature of the mind is pure and is not deluded. Although a person might be very short-tempered and get angry easily, he is not always angry, as long as there is a consciousness. Such an angry person can sometimes also experience love. The basic consciousness of that person is neither anger nor love.

We find that these different aspects of consciousness are temporary and that its basic quality is clarity. This shows that consciousness has the potential to eliminate its delusions, and finally one can establish liberation or nirvana.

How does the scientific mind resolve this concept of no beginning and no end? Is it possible logically?

HH: To understand this, an understanding of the four types of reasoning is required: logical reasoning, the reasoning of functions, the reasoning of dependence, and the reasoning of reality or nature.

For example, if we were to explain why certain substances such as molecules have special powers within themselves, the answer would be that it is their nature. There is no further reason; it is something like a law of nature. On the basis of that, we have the law of dependence. Since there is interdependence of different phenomena because of their aggregations, they have certain functions, certain aspects. On the basis of that, when we are asked why matter is produced as lacking consciousness, lacking knowledge, or why consciousness arises with this quality of clarity, it is just its nature.

But where is the beginning of the beginning of this reality and illusion? If we look at the suffering of humanity, we would have to say that illusion is more common than reality. Why so?

HH: This is explained with ignorance—the first of the Twelve Links of Interdependent Origination. Why does ignorance exist?

The answer is that consciousness has no beginning. If we posit a beginning of the continuity of consciousness, we would have to posit a substantial cause of consciousness that is not consciousness. This is something very important. These are two things: matter and consciousness. These two things are separate entities. However, there is a relationship. Just as matter requires matter for its own substantial cause or main cause, so consciousness requires another consciousness for its substantial cause.

There are broadly two types of causes: the actual cause and conditions—that is, the substantial or main cause—and the cooperative cause. Within the substantial cause, there are again many different causes—for example, direct substantial cause, indirect substantial cause, and so forth. Since consciousness requires another consciousness for the main substantial cause, one has to agree that there is no beginning to these consciousnesses. Since consciousness is beginningless, automatically ignorance is also beginningless.

If one subscribes to the theory of karma for cause and effect, then one must also accept some continuity of consciousness beyond death. How do you explain the relationship between identity and consciousness within the cycle of birth and death?

HH: The answer is ceaseless rebirths. There is a self that is imputed on the basis of this continuity of consciousnesses, which is designated, for example, myself, first a sentient being. In that category all of us are the same, at the same kind of level. Next, I am an Asian. Many are Asians; many are not. Within that, I am a Tibetan, and most of you are not. There are more differences. I am a monk. Within that, the Dalai Lama. So, you see, one being can simultaneously be many.

For example, circumstances might change: if people do not regard me as the Dalai Lama anymore, then that Dalai Lama is no more. But the person is still the same; the monk remains. Then if I disrobed, then I am no more a monk but still a Tibetan, a human being, still a sentient being . . . it works like this.

When death comes, I am no more Tibetan, simultaneously no more a human being, but still the sentient being is there . . . is that clear? So, then in the next birth, I can take human form or animal form. Suppose that consciousness, the sentient being, changes its physical body and is now in animal physical form; that sentient being becomes an animal being. In a subsequent birth that body can change and become a human being . . . it continues like this.

The self is all-pervading, a pervasive self that pervades all lives—past lives, this life, future lives . . . the mere self of the being. There are different types of self: the self that came from past lives, the self that is carried into the next life, the self of this particular life, the self as a monk, and so on—one can make such distinctions.

Your Holiness, is there such a thing as the collective mind or karma? For instance, when groups of people, communities, or nations are suffering, what is the karma?

HH: There are different types of karma, and one of them is collective karma, which we accumulated collectively, and the result of which we have to experience collectively. There are other types of karma that are accumulated individually, and their results have to be experienced individually. The fact that all of us had the possibility to gather here today is the consequence of karma, which we have accumulated collectively. This does not mean that all these karmas were collected together at the same place, at the same time.

Today, you see, the whole Tibetan nation is passing through some kind of suffering. The common cause for this common suffering, I believe, is not necessarily that the present generation committed that karma at one place together, but they may have committed that same amount of karma at different places, at different times. Because of their common suffering, at times it is entirely possible that karma might have been committed in the past collectively by a community.

For example, in the First World War, millions of people were involved. There were many people making weapons with a kind of common intention or motivation. So that creates common karma.

Couldn't the theory of karma be used to justify existing aggressiveness, cruelty, or injustice and to covet one's own privileged position?

HH: I think that, in some cases, this possibility exists. There is a big social gap today. Some people are very poor, some wealthy. It does not help for us to say to those who are poor or in grave difficulty that it is a consequence of their karma. Of course, we must ultimately ask who created the karma. *We ourselves!* Today's experiences happen due to our past karma. We created karma; karma is in our own hands, on our own shoulders.

Just because we have no memory of our past actions that have created our present circumstances, it does not mean that we are not responsible for them. In fact, we must always react with compassion to help those who suffer. Once we exhaust our own good karma, our own suffering could increase and we could be in a similar position to theirs. By selflessly helping others, we can accumulate positive karma ourselves.

Issues such as contraception and abortion are controversial both when practiced as social policy, as in China, or as a matter of personal choice in liberal societies. How do you view this in karmic terms?

HH: In order to have a better human society—better standards of living—some kind of planning, of population control, is necessary. Whether it is right or wrong depends on the motivation. If the population goes out of control, the result is more suffering. With good motivation and a concern for the welfare of human beings, it is right to work toward reducing suffering.

CHAPTER 8

REINCARNATION

You are regarded by millions as the reincarnation of Avalokiteshvara, the Buddha of Compassion. Are you consciously aware that you are a reincarnation of Avalokiteshvara?

HH: Of Avalokiteshvara? No, no, no! That, I think, is a little bit of an exaggeration. I always describe myself as a Buddhist monk.

Of course, I believe that with the previous—the first Dalai Lama, the second, and I think up to the seventh Dalai Lama—there are clear indications. They are, what you say, reincarnations of Avalokiteshvara—especially the first and the second. For myself, I do not believe I am of the original Dalai Lama. But I do feel that I have a special relationship with the 5th and the 13th Dalai Lamas.

There are different types of reincarnation. In some cases, it's the same person or same being. In other cases, it's not the same being, but someone else who has come in his or her place. In some, the reincarnation has come as a relative.

If you ask me whether I am the reincarnation of Dalai Lama, my answer is yes, but not necessarily in the sense that I came in the tenth Dalai Lama's place to fulfill his work.

Your Holiness, with your pursuit of the scientific method, logical analysis, and rationality, how do you reconcile with being a reincarnation?

HH: There are various interpretations of reincarnation. For myself, I think it means deliberately taking birth in order to succeed in what was started in a previous life or to complete the work of someone else's previous life. In that sense, I feel I am an incarnation.

Moreover, as a Buddhist, or as a Buddhist who continues to study Buddhist logic and Buddhist philosophy, if it is scientifically proved that certain things do not exist, then theoretically speaking, it has to be accepted. For example, if reincarnation is thoroughly investigated in a scientific way and it is proved 100 percent that it doesn't exist, theoretically speaking, Buddhists would have to accept that.

But you must see the difference between merely not *finding* proof and having tangible proof that something *doesn't* exist. From the Buddhist point of view, also, if something cannot be found through philosophy, it doesn't mean it doesn't exist. We believe it does exist, but finding it depends on many factors.

Do you feel you are the reincarnation of the 13th Dalai Lama, and is there "incomplete" work for you to complete?

HH: I must answer that with both a yes and a no. In my dream state, I met the 13th Dalai Lama three times. I don't believe that I am necessarily the same being. I feel, however, that I have a very strong karmic link with him. The 13th Dalai Lama made progress in both the temporal and spiritual fields. However, we also believe that he had a more long-term plan for his work that would overlap beyond his lifetime. He died in his late 50s, and the work that he had begun was neither fulfilled nor completed.

Do you know that for sure?

HH: Not very sure. But it is what I feel.

The physical body decays upon death, so is it the mind or the consciousness that is reincarnated?

HH: First, you must ask yourself the basic question "What is 'self' or 'I'?" Certainly, this body is not the central being, and the mind alone is also not a central being. For me, Tenzin Gyatso is the human being. However, from the Buddhist point of view, in the Mahayana system, they say the central being, Tenzin Gyatso, is designated here as the human being and is the combination of this body and mind. This body comes from parents and is subject to various causes and conditions.

The being is chosen because of a combination of the body and the mind, and also the subtle level of the body and the grosser level of the mind. The process for rebirth is the continuation of the mind or the continuation of the being. Reincarnation is a deliberate birth at a certain time, in a certain area. It could be the same person and the same being, or a different person who has come to fulfill his previous unfinished work.

Ultimately, some Buddhist scriptures say that the space particle is the original cause of this body, and that particle was also the cause for the whole previous universe. But consciousness or mind is changing every moment. Therefore, it can be shown that causes and conditions will affect anything that undergoes change. As such, the mind is also a product of causes and conditions. That is the basis of the rebirth theory.

Currently, do you have any memories of your past life?

HH: Sometimes it is difficult to remember what happened this morning! However, when I was small— say, two to three years old—my mother and some close friends noticed that I expressed some memories of my past life. That is possible! But if you are asking me for a definite memory, I must say it remains somewhat unclear.

If Buddhism is open to scientific questioning, why does the belief in reincarnation still survive? There is no supporting science or reason for this.

HH: Science, as we know it, involves investigation of something that can be measured or calculated. The concept of mind or the concept of self itself cannot be measured. Up to now, the scientific field from the Buddhist viewpoint has been limited, I think. Mind and consciousness are outside the present scientific field. Because there have been many sophisticated experiments on the brain about the experience of dying people, these perhaps may lead to a wider field. But at the same time, we must appreciate what science has not found or says is nonexistent.

Your Holiness, would that not be the case with incarnate lamas who to some degree have recollections of past lives?

HH: This is not necessarily only a Buddhist concept. In fact, there are two girls in two families near Palampur and in Ambala [in north India]. About two years ago, I sent some people to investigate because at that time the girls, who were four or five, talked very clearly about their past lives, and each claimed that the other girl's parents were her own. As a result, these two girls now have four parents each—parents in this life and parents from a past life. Their recollections were so convincing that each set of parents accepted the other girl as their own child.

I studied a similar case where a little boy claimed that he had a wife and children, and his parents beat him, saying he was a liar. Eventually, by chance, a visitor from the village where he claimed to have a family mentioned that there were people by the same names that he was talking about. So, they took the child to the other village, where he identified a lady as his wife from among three or four women and talked about his children!

Do you think about your reincarnation in your next life?

HH: Of course! The words of Shantideva were, "As long as space remains, as long as suffering of sentient beings remains, I will remain in order to serve, in order to work for them." That verse gives me the inner strength, hope, and a defined purpose of my being.

I am definitely ready as long as my reincarnation is of some benefit, some usefulness. I'm quite sure I will take rebirth. In what place, in what form, or with what name, I don't know. But the reincarnation of the Dalai Lama is a different matter. The time may come when the institution of the Dalai Lama may no longer be beneficial and there would be no reason for it to continue. On this, I remain open.

As far as my rebirth is concerned, until Buddhahood is reached, I firmly believe my rebirth is always there. Even after Buddhahood, I will continue somewhere in different manifestations. That is the Buddhist belief, the Buddhist thinking. I really feel that a teaching of this kind sustains one's optimism, will, and determination.

The need for birth control is justified by the finite resources of our planet, which cannot sustain an infinitely growing population. Some people believe we are thus denying large numbers of sentient beings birth in human form. What do you think?

HH: This can be summed up in a comment by Gandhiji: there is enough for everybody's need, but not for everybody's greed. This balances out the karmic concept of reincarnation. The world has enough to feed everybody if the divisions were better and people did not tend to accumulate more than they should. These two theories balance out to some degree if one could in that sense distribute the well-being of others. There is so much food being destroyed, dumped into the ocean, while millions of people are going hungry. This, I think, is in part both moral and karmic weakness.

I think the confusion is about what is reborn. Is it the entity, the identity? Does it become part of a larger consciousness, part of which manifests itself again? I think that is the area of confusion. It also includes the notion that a number of souls are waiting to be reborn. That suggests the notion that there are that many different entities or identities waiting to be reborn. If we understand the "I" correctly, our responses change.

But I do not know who that "I" is. If I am born again, I do not remember what I was before! Unless I am conscious that it is me, what difference does it make?

HH: Whose continuity of consciousness is it? To whom does it belong? The answer to the question is that it belongs to the being himself. Whether one can find that self—"I"—or not is a different question altogether. If one were to say my previous life is my own being, one has to recollect it. Then it is not unrecognized. We can recognize certain experiences; others, even of this life, we cannot. On this basis, we cannot say that was not me.

In other words, there are people who very clearly remember past lives. But ordinary people cannot remember past lives because the level of consciousness during the time of death, the interval state between the previous life and the next life, is most subtle. When that happens, the gross level of mind on which those memories are based cannot function well. A person who has some experience of utilizing deeper consciousnesses has a better chance of having clearer memories of past lives.

Please explain what happens to the mind at the time of death, or what is it that moves from one incarnation to the next and carries forward the karmic imprints?

HH: That depends on the previous lives—the mental capacity through samadhi or mental training. Some memories, some sustainable experiences, and other mental qualities of the past life remain intact in the next. But the body changes, as does the grosser level of mind, so that in the next life there are not so many traces present. But then again, there is always some kind of small influence or imprint from the previous life.

At the time of death, there are practices and trainings in the Tibetan tradition that teach you how to manage and how to direct the subtle mind. So once the gross body and the gross mind have fallen away, what is it that directs the mind to a suitable incarnation in the next life?

HH: It depends very much on the quality or the experience carried forward by the subtle mind. Those experiences that have a closer relation with the subtle mind have a greater possibility of being transmitted to the next life. This continuation or transmigration of the subtle mind, in fact, is a kind of natural process; and likewise the "self" is being designated on the subtle mind, and the transference of that "self" to the next life is also a kind of natural process. As explained earlier, whether that mind carries with it a positive imprint or negative imprint depends very much on the kind of life lived in the previous life, or karma.

Consciousness requires a substantial cause, an earlier moment of consciousness. This basic reason proves the existence of rebirth. If we look further for the continuity of consciousness of this life, like the time of conception, then this continuity can be traced to the previous life. In that case, there is no reason why the continuity of consciousness should cease at the last moment of this life, at the time of death.

For this reason, we have to be concerned about our future lives. Whether we will have good or unfortunate future lives depends on our actions in this life. While we are busy in this life, we should not neglect to think about future lives.

Then there is another aspect. Everybody wants happiness, and nobody wants suffering. If material progress could provide the complete happiness we are seeking, there should be people in this world who are totally satisfied and who should not have even the slightest experience of suffering. However, as long as we have this physical body, the potential for suffering will always exist; this is the nature of samsara. Birth into this body is the basis of misfortune. If we have the possibility to cease rebirth, this is something worthwhile to achieve. This we call *moksha* or liberation.

Would you say that you would be ready to disbelieve in reincarnation if the proof were there?

HH: Oh yes. I think, strictly speaking, from the Buddhist viewpoint, if scientific experiment or investigation convincingly shows with 100 percent certainty that there is no continuation of mind, then of course, we have to accept it. Normally, when we investigate something, we consider the reasons for establishing that point and whether we accept any opposing factors. The rebirth theory involves two things: one, even today there are people who have a clear memory about their past life; and the other, if there is no continuity of life, how does the whole world or universe exist?

There must be some causes. The concept of the Creator raised many contradictions; therefore, at least for Buddhists, it seems more comfortable to accept the theory of rebirth—that the beginning of life is due to their actions, so the whole universe comes and goes, comes and goes. But there always remains an element of mystery.

So according to the theory of karma, because of the number of mosquitoes I have killed in this life, I will have to be reborn a mosquito . . .

HH: As far as that is concerned, unless I do some special method of purification, well . . . otherwise, I remember very clearly that I have sinned. I have killed mosquitoes on one occasion in Lhasa, in Tibet; then on another occasion in south India, I killed a few mosquitoes. Those actions are quite enough to take rebirth as a mosquito.

Does every karma find the physical or external conditions in this world to balance or complete it?

HH: If, for example, someone has accumulated the karma to take rebirth as a human being on this planet, but because of some external circumstances this planet has been destroyed or has yet to be evolved and such, in these circumstances either his karmic action will have to wait for its maturation or he will take rebirth on another planet that has identical form. To take rebirth into a specific form does require external conditions for the existence of that specific form. Two things are necessary: in order to take rebirth as a human being, karma alone is not enough; one also needs parents.

Is it necessary to believe in future and past lives?

HH: If we do not adhere to the theory of rebirth or do not accept past lives, we have to set some point of beginning for beings.

I usually say that whether you are a believer or nonbeliever, you should be a kindhearted person. That can be developed without acceptance of past or future lives or without the acceptance of Buddhist or karmic theory. This is religion in itself.

I strongly feel that even antireligious people—like Communists, for example—can be very good-hearted, as I have personally experienced. People with good hearts do exist without any Buddhist theory of rebirth—those who sacrifice their own lives for the benefit of the masses either through their inborn qualities or in another way.

Love and kindness are a universal religion. Today we are discussing Buddhism, so I am talking about these things from the Buddhist point of view. If someone without these practices simply tries to be a good person, that is certainly possible and he will succeed. If, however, a person does not accept the existence of a completely enlightened state, then the question of bodhicitta does not arise either, because it is a state of mind that aspires to Buddhahood. That is some kind of process in the Buddhist point of view.

There is one question that many people ask. If Buddhists don't believe in an <u>atman</u>—the self or soul—what is it that reincarnates?

HH: Buddhists emphasize *anatman,* and much is dependent on the connotation or understanding of the meaning of the term *anatman,* or selflessness. Sometimes confusion arises due to the usage of the word in different contexts. So, when we talk about anatman, we do not mean the total nonexistence of the nominal or conventional self; we very much accept the existence of such a conventional self. What we actually mean is the nonexistence of the self that is thought to be totally independent and has nothing whatsoever to do with the self of the physical aggregates; it is totally separate from the self of the physical aggregates, which is the kind of self that is being denied.

When we talk of past and future lives with conviction, there must be some energy or something that comes from past lives and enters this physical body and goes from this life to the next one, leaving this physical body behind. And that something must be separate from this physical body.

According to some Buddhist schools, it is believed that between the mind and the body—since the physical body is only for this life—it must be the mind that goes from one life to another. But the mind is also heavily entangled with various senses and organs, which are again very physical and confined to just one life. Therefore, it must be a very subtle mind. That must be the self. This is one Buddhist school of thought—*chitta*. Even in chitta there are different levels. So, ultimately, a subtler chitta is the self.

Yet another Buddhist school of thought argues that even the subtle mind, no matter *how* subtle, cannot be considered as "my" mind. Therefore, that mind itself is self. If the mind becomes the self, both the ownership and what is owned by that owner become one.

If death is the ultimate state of consciousness, then what about ghosts? Have you ever come across any?

HH: I do remember that, as a child, I was very scared of ghosts.

In Buddhism, we have six types of rebirths. This division is made on the basis of the degree of suffering or pleasure. When the division is made on the basis of having gross or subtle levels of form, feeling, or mind, we divide sentient beings into three realms. This is further divided into three: 6 types of *devas* [supernatural beings] belonging to the desire realm, 16 types belonging to the form realm, and 4 types belonging to the formless realm. So we have here three realms: desire realm, form realm, and formless realm.

Ghosts can belong to any of these three realms or states. Some are positive and some negative; just like human beings, some are very cruel and some are very kind—it is like that.

CHAPTER 9

NIRVANA/MOKSHA

Your Holiness, nirvana as a phenomenon has been a unique and revolutionary gift of Buddhism as a wisdom school. It is also the one concept that became the raison d'être of what we call Buddhahood, the legend of Buddha, and his divergence from the traditional concept of God. Could you please clarify for us what is meant by nirvana?

HH: Buddhist explanations say that beings are not derived from a pure source free of all delusions. As explained earlier, ignorance has no beginning, so suffering has no beginning either; and samsara, cyclic existence, has no beginning. Achieving nirvana means that an individual gets to the stage where his mind is free of all delusion, and that stage is called liberation.

Ultimately, nirvana has to be explained from the viewpoint of emptiness, through the cessation of suffering, which is the reality, which is the expanse of phenomena into which all these delusions are purged or purified. It is not just an emptiness, but the emptiness of a mind free of all delusions. This emptiness is like the quality of *being* emptiness as samsara, which is also in the nature of emptiness. In that respect, there is no difference between samsara and nirvana.

Is nirvana, then, an inherent state awaiting discovery or the ultimate potential?

HH: When we talk of delusions, or the faults of the mind, as being temporary, it explains implicitly that there is a possibility of being freed from them. We have that potential, but we do not have nirvana in ourselves.

Dharmakirti says, in Pramanavarttika, that the mere presence of the ultimate cause would require the presence of effect or proof. When we say that on a blade of grass there is an insect that has the karmic potential of taking rebirth as an elephant a hundred times, we would also have to say that on that blade of grass there are a hundred elephants.

Buddha nature is the potential that is inherent in everybody's consciousness and which, when activated by circumstances, can be fully realized; but it is not the Buddha himself.

The path, the quality of nirvana being empty of inherent existence . . . that nature is there within us. At least the potential of it is in our mind—and not only the potential, the *thing* is there; *we* are there. Naturally it exists due to some other factor. There is no independent existence.

Absence of independent existence is ultimate nature—*shunyata*. Shunyata is there. Phenomena that exist in dependence on other factors are devoid of an independent self. Therefore, these are all part of emptiness. And reaching that ultimate state of realization—we are all part of emptiness—is our potential and nirvana.

But in a state of nirvana does one still respond to phenomena?

HH: There is still the distinction between bad and good, negative and positive. Accordingly, we feel *This is something good; that is something bad,* of course. Within enlightenment, the highest form is Buddhahood, in which even appearances of true existence are prevented.

At one time, I think in the late '60s or early '70s, I meditated quite intensely on shunyata. One day I found a teaching by Je Tsongkhapa in which he said, "The collection of the aggregates is not the self, the continuity of the collection of the aggregates, none of these are self." When I read that statement, I got quite frightened. Actually, this was an explanation of the essence of one of the teachings of the Indian master Nagarjuna, which says:

A person is not the earth element,
Nor the water element, nor the fire element,
Nor the wind element.
At the same, there is no person who is
Apart from them.

It also says that if you analytically search for it, it is not findable. I gained some small understanding or realization, and in the next few days, I gained a different feeling or attitude toward different objects.

How would you define <u>nirvana</u> or <u>enlightenment</u> to the Western mind that leans toward seeing matter, which you call delusory, as the primary force of existence—identifiable and provable?

HH: The West really has much knowledge about matter, yet Western knowledge on consciousness seems very limited. It is at the beginner's stage. Without a deep knowledge of consciousness, even a full knowledge of matter is questionable.

In any case, since knowledge is acquired not by sentient beings generally but by human beings, the main purpose of acquiring this knowledge is to benefit humanity. If that is so, it is very important to have balanced knowledge, knowledge of/through inner experience—mainly consciousness—and the knowledge of matter/material, as they go together. If we have that kind of balanced approach, it makes a lot of difference, without losing the identity or characteristics of a human being.

But if we approach scientific research purely with one-sided knowledge and do not take the fact of internal consciousness into consideration, the scientist automatically neglects the experience of feeling; he automatically neglects something.

If our whole approach concentrates only on the material side and completely ignores consciousness, there is no demarcation between justice and injustice, right and wrong. I think that Western society simply concentrates too much on material development. The whole of human energy is spent on matter, and consciousness is neglected. This will result in unpleasant experiences. A balance would make a happier society.

I believe that the discussion or study of consciousness is not necessarily a religious matter but simply important for technical knowledge, human knowledge. I think this subject is very important. In that respect, Eastern philosophy—especially Buddhist philosophy—has something to contribute to the West.

If you were to break down the path to nirvana into stages, how would you define the first stage?

HH: In order to achieve liberation, first of all, one must develop a strong wish to achieve it. Aryadeva said in his Four Hundred Verses that for someone who has no reversed attitude toward worldly possessions, there is no possibility of achieving liberation. Therefore, it is necessary to identify and reflect on suffering. The chief suffering we are referring to is the suffering of conditioning.

Our aggregates are impermanent—that is, they are subject to change. They are the product of cause; and cause, in this case, refers to the contaminated actions we have committed—that is, karma, and also the delusions that induced it. Because form is the product of this impermanence, it is in the nature of suffering.

There are many different ways to contemplate the suffering of birth. Prior to birth, after having ceased the intermediate state and arisen in the Clear Light, there are no obvious sufferings, and feelings are neutralized. During conception and after entering the womb, the process of physical development begins. The form becomes grosser and grosser, and at a certain stage one starts to experience pleasure and pain and so on. At the time of actual birth, real suffering begins. Starting from that point until a certain period of time, we remain as helpless as an infant insect. This is how our lives begin.

Rationally speaking, our body is not at all an object worthy to be cherished or attached to. Its substances are unclean. The body itself is unclean and is the product of unclean bodies. The cause of this body is the two regenerative fluids of the parents, which are also unclean.

To speak of what the body produces, it produces feces and urine. That is the main purpose of the body—to consume food and drink and to produce human waste. If I think of the amount of food and drink I have consumed up to now, I feel I have consumed quite a lot. At the same time, discharges, such as mucus and the like, all put together are also quite a lot.

And on top of that, with this physical human body, we are cheating, bullying people, creating problems. Just what is the value of this life?! If we think of this, life is very saddening. No matter how beautiful or strong the body is, its real substances such as skin, flesh, and so forth are not beautiful, but impure.

Nobody regards the toilet as something clean, do they? But actually one's body is a toilet. The things inside us do not come from the sky; they come from the body—so what is the point of feeling attachment for the body? In itself, it is not sacred.

Fortunately, with this body we have the human mind. We are able to think and analyze many things, and that is the only worthwhile part. With the power of our intelligence, we can make our lives purposeful.

Animals and insects can develop a limited kind of altruism. Bees and ants, for example, are very social insects, and they have a sense of responsibility and genuine cooperation in good or bad times. This is their social structure. Human nature is also like that. We cannot survive alone; we have to depend on others, whether we like it or not.

Yes, I see—detachment from the physical body is the first realization. But how does one train this mind to move from attachment to altruism?

HH: The Indian masters developed two major systems for the training and development of an altruistic mind: the *Seven-Point Cause-and-Effect Method* and the *Exchange and Equalizing of Oneself with Others*. These days, when we undertake the practice of cultivating bodhicitta, we combine the two systems.

— The first of the seven points is the cultivation of equanimity—that is, a state of mind that tries to equalize the strong attachment to friends, the strong hatred for enemies, and an indifferent attitude toward neutral people.

— The second stage is remembering our own beginningless rebirths so that we can recognize that all sentient beings have been our mothers, friends, and relatives at one time or another.

— Third, having recognized them as such, we recollect and reflect on the kindnesses they extended to us. This attitude—the special recollection of kindnesses—does not discriminate between friends and enemies; even enemies are regarded as very kind.

— The next step is to repay their kindnesses by reflecting how our mother of this lifetime extends her kindness to us and how other parents extend their kindness to their children.

— Then comes the stage of loving-kindness. This is a state of mind that cherishes all sentient beings. Having developed this loving-kindness for all sentient beings, we wish that all sentient beings be free from suffering. That is compassion.

— This is followed by an unusual attitude in which we take upon ourselves the responsibility to free all sentient beings from suffering.

— And the final stage is actual bodhicitta, the altruistic attitude to achieve enlightenment. This is experienced partly by the force of our strong compassion for all sentient beings, the feeling of being able to see their suffering, and partly by the understanding that it is possible for the mind of a sentient being to be freed from its delusions. All sentient beings have the potential to achieve the omniscient state. Understanding this, combined with a strong force of compassion, brings about the experience of bodhicitta.

This is the Seven-Point Cause-and-Effect Method.
The second system is also the cultivation of equanimity, but in a different way.

— All sentient things are equal in their wish for happiness and desire to avoid suffering. Knowing this is like equalizing oneself with others.

— Next is the reflection on the disadvantages of cherishing oneself. Although a very selfish person is so because he wants all the happiness for himself, all he gets in the end is many enemies and few friends. On the other hand, if we cherish others instead of cherishing ourselves, we will experience the opposite result—more friends and fewer enemies.

In short, just as Shantideva said in his Bodhicaryavatara, all frustrations you find in this world are the product of selfish thought, and all the happiness you find is the product of cherishing others. This is a reflection on the disadvantages of self-cherishing and the advantages of cherishing others. Through this, one engages in exchanging oneself with others.

— The next step is the practice of giving and taking, and then follows the actual cultivation of bodhicitta.

In order to develop genuine altruism, you need to control anger and hatred. In order to do that, you need the practice of patience and tolerance—without that, you cannot control anger. In order to develop patience and tolerance, you need an enemy. Without an enemy, you cannot develop these qualities. That is the point. If you think like this, you really make use of the enemy, irrespective of his motivations.

As far as I am concerned, enemies have been very helpful. When one is capable of seeing them as helpful and kind, there is no question of seeing them as before, as enemies. Our greatest stumbling block is our enemy. When we focus on that obstacle—the enemy—everything else becomes very easy.

Viewing our enemy as a teacher is indeed an advanced stage of altruism. How does one control the obsessive selfishness of the delusory mind so that it can begin to value altruism in the first place?

HH: All worldly desires—such as fame, wealth, health, and the like—depend on the kindness of others. They are fulfilled in dependence on others. Even the possibility of us coming together here and having this comfortable discussion was brought about through the contribution of many others—those who built this house, wove the carpets . . . the bus by which you came. All these factors brought us here together. Without these, we would not have had the opportunity to meet. There are known and unknown people involved, and without their involvement, we could not have met.

Think along these lines and you will develop the conviction that without the help of others, you cannot survive. Think also about karma: the chance of having this good opportunity is the product of our own virtuous actions in the past. Think about what is meant by virtuous karma. It means something we have done with the motivation of helping others. Thus, even the accumulation of virtuous karma requires others as its basis.

Your Holiness, Buddhism as a religion and you in particular hold bodhicitta as the superlative path to liberation. Why is that?

HH: Of all the Buddhist practices, bodhicitta is regarded as the most precious. Bodhicitta has its root in compassion. Without suffering sentient beings, we cannot develop compassion. We cannot cultivate compassion by focusing on the Buddha; it is only possible to develop compassion by focusing on suffering sentient beings. The direct cause of bodhicitta is possible only by focusing on sentient beings. We may get blessings from the Buddha for the development of bodhicitta. From this point of view, we find that sentient beings are kinder than the Buddha. It is not necessary for the other sentient beings to have good motivation on their part. The objects which we regard as valuable and cherish—for example, cessation and the paths—do not have good motivations, but we cherish and value them.

We talked about the unusual attitude of becoming responsible for freeing sentient beings from suffering. Bodhicitta, induced by this unusual attitude, is very powerful. This is the combined practice of the two systems we earlier discussed: the Seven-Point Cause-and-Effect Method and the Exchange and Equalizing of Oneself with Others. This useful and effective practice gives you inner strength, tranquility, and a warm heart. Such an attitude is the real refuge. Even a little experience as a result of this practice gives you inner peace and strength.

Isn't bodhicitta as the central teaching of Buddhism, then, the perfect formula for ensuring world peace and a more humane world?

HH: Yes. People who do not accept the existence of a next life or nirvana are all right as long as they remain good members of human society. They, too, have to practice these things because it is of benefit to the mind. That is the first step toward the development of genuine, lasting world peace. External peace cannot be developed without internal peace—this is really a profound teaching and advice.

For the practitioner of the bodhisattva, all sentient beings are his friends, and all environments are conducive to his practice. The actual enemies for him are a selfish attitude within himself, his self-grasping attitude, and his distorted views. When one practices in such a way, one is not free from all fear. But, at least at the level of one's mind, one gains a certain kind of peace and freedom from fear. This is how one cultivates the aspiration to achieve liberation and the aspiration to achieve the omniscient state.

Your Holiness, what would be your explanation or understanding of, or insight into, mystical experience in the Buddhist tradition?

HH: Even a genuine practitioner can experience different kinds of mystical experiences. At the initial stage, these experiences are not at all reliable. So if he or she is too attached or considers these as important or a great experience, it is absolutely wrong. There is great danger in doing so.

Once you further your own mental development through practice, what for you is merely a manifestation or reflection of your deeper experience, looks like a mystical experience to ordinary people. But it is normal for you. So I think we have to make this distinction.

Your Holiness, nirvana, moksha, enlightenment, and Buddhahood are terms that have come into common usage, yet their meanings are far from clear. For instance, what happens to the "mind" in these states?

HH: According to Buddhist philosophy, when the person or the "self" is still there, the mind is still there, even up to Buddhahood. At the Buddha stage, also, the individual identity is still there. According to another school of thought, the highest state is one where the person ceases to exist and the mind also ceases. If that is true, I prefer not to attain nirvana; I prefer this life to a state where there is no feeling, because I don't think that state is something positive.

For example, according to Vaibhasika—a Buddhist school—Mahaparinirvana is a state not only free of mental delusions but also free of the mind itself. No continuity of the mind exists. According to them, Buddha Shakyamuni is only a historical figure. He does not exist anymore.

Nagarjuna refuted this, asserting that if ultimate nirvana is also free of mind, where is the person who actualizes this state? We have to believe, have to agree, that someone achieves this state of nirvana. There should be a person who achieves it.

If we say nirvana or liberation is a state where the mind is completely free of delusion, it does not mean that the mind itself has also ceased. There is something, something positive, isn't there? If we achieved that kind of nirvana, we would be very happy, wouldn't we? But if nirvana were completely nothingness, if everything discontinued, we would prefer not to achieve it, wouldn't we?

Is nirvana a state of nonfeeling or a state of different kind of feeling?

HH: Oh yes, a different kind of feeling.

What is different about that kind of feeling?

HH: That is difficult to say, I think—first let me achieve it . . . [laughter]. Mainly, of course, it is a feeling of realization. The entire attitude toward phenomena changes completely. Now we have anger, attachment, and all these negative thoughts and emotions. With our negative thoughts, we cannot see or realize actual reality. Our perspective is colored. Due to ignorance, grasping at true existence, everything appears as if it existed on its own—that very strong, solid appearance is also there. When we reach nirvana, these negative or distorted thoughts are completely purified; and as a result, the whole attitude toward phenomena is different.

Your Holiness, the Buddha did not answer some questions because he was omniscient. Your Holiness did not answer my question about the possibility of laughing our way to nirvana. Was that for the same reason?

HH: I did not understand your question, not because I am omniscient but because I have *obscuration* to knowledge.

CHAPTER 10

CONSCIOUSNESS

Consciousness continues to be a complex phenomenon for the modern mind, whether we approach it through science or spirituality. Your Holiness, could you clarify how Buddhism defines consciousness?

HH: Consciousness is generally divided into two: sensory consciousness and mental consciousness. The arising of sensory consciousness such as eye-consciousness depends on certain conditions—for instance, the objective condition or the internal condition that is the empowering condition. On the basis of these two, the sense organ also requires another factor—that is, the preceding moment of the consciousness itself.

Let us talk on the basis of this flower, the eye-consciousness that sees the flower. The function of the objective condition, which is the flower, is that it can produce the eye-consciousness that brings forth awareness of the different aspects of the flower.

Vaibhasika, one of the Buddhist schools, does not accept the theory of aspect. It says eye-consciousness has direct contact with the object itself. This is very difficult to explain. It says that things are perceived without aspect but by direct contact. Other schools say that things do have aspects through which the consciousness perceives the object.

The theory of modern scientists, which accepts the aspect of the object through which it is perceived, seems to have a more logical background. The eye-consciousness perceives a form, and not a sound, that is the imprint of the sense organ on which it depends. What is the cause that produces such an eye-consciousness in the nature of clarity and knowing? That is the product of the preceding moment of the consciousness that gives rise to the eye-consciousness.

Although we talk about states in which gross levels of mind are dissolved, and we talk of consciousness states and so on, the subtle consciousness always retains its continuity. If one of the conditions—for example, the preceding moment of the consciousness—is not complete, even when the sense organ and the object meet, they will not be able to produce the eye-consciousness that sees it.

Mental consciousness is very different, and the ways in which the sensory and mental consciousnesses perceive an object are also very different. Because sensory consciousness is nonconceptual, it perceives all the qualities—all the attributes of the object—collectively.

When we talk about mental consciousness, it is mainly conceptual. It perceives an object through an image. It apprehends an object by excluding what it is not. One has really to think deeply about the question of whether consciousnesses are created or produced from chemical particles of the brain mechanism.

As a spiritual leader you have taken unprecedented initiative in involving the scientific community in testing, analyzing, and validating spiritual phenomena. Yet the mind and the brain are as far as scientists are willing to explore. What is their stand on consciousness, and how does it differ from yours?

HH: In recent years, I met scientists in the fields of nuclear physics as well as neurology and psychology. Very interesting. We have to learn certain things from their experiments, from their latest findings; and, equally, they show a keen interest to know more about Buddhist explanations of consciousness and mind.

I have raised this question with many people but have never found a satisfactory answer. For example, if we adhere to a position that consciousness is nothing other than a product of the interaction of particles within the brain, we have to say that each consciousness is produced from particles in the brain.

In that case, take the possible experiences in relation to a rose. One person might have the view that this is a plastic rose—that is a mistaken consciousness. Later, he might doubt it, thinking that it might not be a plastic rose, so the mistaken consciousness now turns into a wavering doubt. Then he presumes that it is a natural flower—this is still only a presumption. Finally, through some circumstances, such as touching it or smelling it, he finds that it is a natural rose.

During all these stages, his consciousness is directed toward one single object, but he is passing through these different stages of consciousness: from the mistaken view to doubt, then presumption, and finally from valid cognition to valid perception. He is experiencing different stages of consciousness. But how does one explain that the chemical particles change during these stages?

Another example: We see a person and think he is our friend. But that person is not our friend. We mistake him, and the consciousness is mistaken. When we saw that person, we had an erroneous consciousness. But the moment someone told us that he was not our friend, hearing this sound caused a change from that mistaken perception of the person to a valid perception.

What about the experiences of great meditators? When a practitioner enters a very deep state of meditation, both breathing and heartbeat stop. Some of my friends who practice these things remain without heartbeat and breathing for a few minutes, I think. If someone remains in such a state for a few hours, what is the function of the brain during that time?

On the basis of all this, I am trying to argue that there exists one phenomenon, called consciousness, that has its own entity apart from the brain cells. Although the gross level of consciousness is very closely related to the physical body, it is also naturally related to the brain. But the consciousness of its own nature is something distinct. The subtler consciousness becomes more independent of the physical particles.

That is how the physical functions of a meditator stop when he reaches a deep state of consciousness; yet consciousness is there. At that moment, because the physical functions have stopped, the gross level of consciousness is no more and the subtle level of consciousness becomes obvious.

So is consciousness a phenomenon of many layers? For instance, what state does one experience in death?

HH: There are different states of consciousnesses: the waking state, the dream state, very deep sleep, and the state of unconsciousness—for example, in a faint, the subtlest level of consciousness.

According to the highest Yogatantra, the actual process of death is preceded by eight dissolution processes—that is, the dissolution of the elements of earth, water, fire, wind, and space. We then go through processes known as appearances: red increase, black near attainment, and Clear Light of Death. Some people experience these dissolutions up to a certain stage and then turn back. I have met people who experienced this and were fascinated by these unusual events.

According to the highest Buddhist tantra, they seem to have experienced a certain deep level of consciousness and then returned. When, after the experience of the Clear Light of Death, someone is taking birth into a realm where there is an intermediate state, or *bardo,* he goes through this intermediate stage. When, for example, the being is taking rebirth as a human, he experiences the intermediate state before the consciousness enters the womb. The process is the same for test-tube babies. In any case, the life process begins and ends with the experience of the Clear Light.

If we do not accept the continuity of consciousness, the big question is: *how did the world evolve?* If we accept the big bang theory, what was the reason for the big bang to have happened? It is evident that the whole system of the universe first evolves, then remains, and finally disappears. If we adhere to a position in which we say that things can exist without any cause, we find many logical inconsistencies. But if, on the other hand, we accept a cause, we have to accept the theory of a Creator. In this case, too, there arise a lot of logical inconsistencies.

According to the Buddhist point of view, since sentient beings take part in the environment or natural habitat, the universe evolves. This means, if we accept the beginningless continuity of consciousness, there is some way to explain the cycle of life. Although such a position poses fewer questions, some questions still arise. For example, why does consciousness have no beginning?

If we accept the continuity of consciousness and that of sentient beings, or life, there are fewer questions. So we prefer not a full answer but less controversy. We accept that there is no beginning and no end of subtle consciousness. In enlightenment, Buddhahood, subtle consciousness still exists; there is no end.

How would you distinguish between what we know as the cognitive mind and consciousness?

HH: There are two types of mental consciousnesses: conceptual and nonconceptual. Nonconceptual mental consciousness is also known as direct perception. All Buddhist schools accept three direct perceptions: *sensorial; mental;* and *yogic,* achieved through meditation.

There are the six primary consciousnesses, ranging from visual consciousness to that of the mind. All of them have accompanying mental factors—the five ever-functioning mental factors, and those that are sometimes present and sometimes not. The sutras explain that the eye-consciousness sees a form, but it is not aware of the fact that it is form. Due to different functions, consciousnesses are divided into two: valid cognition and invalid cognition.

In order to achieve the desired results, we have to follow valid cognition. The results of valid cognition may be uninterrupted or interrupted. There are three types of invalid cognition: *nonperception of the object, mistaken consciousness,* and *doubt:*

- **Nonperception** includes consciousness that has the appearance of the object but cannot register it, cannot recognize it. It also includes consciousness that is mere assumption.

- **Mistaken consciousness** distorts the object it holds.

- There are three kinds of **doubt** or wavering consciousness: one tends to gravitate toward the truth, one toward wrong perception, and the third is equally balanced between the two.

There are different levels of invalid cognition. In order to counteract them, there are different stages of the transformation of consciousness. At the first stage, one has to counteract the single-pointed, mistaken view. For this, there are methods such as syllogisms by which one shows one's own position and shatters the force of the single-pointed, mistaken view.

After the force of single-pointedness has gone comes the stage of doubt and more doubt. These are overcome by the use of syllogisms and logical reasoning. An inferential understanding of the object is gained, and when we develop familiarity with that object, we reach the stage in which consciousness becomes nonconceptual.

There are three types of wisdom: that which arises from mere listening, from contemplation, and from meditation. These are just basic explanations of consciousnesses.

In order to understand the presentation of consciousness in detail, one has first to understand the presentation of the different objects of consciousness, the agents by which one knows these different presentations, and the way in which the consciousness cooperates with the object. There are different ways in which consciousnesses engage with their objects.

For nonconceptual consciousness, there is what is called the appearing object, but no object of conceptualization as in conceptual thought. For conceptual thought, there is what is called the object of conceptualization. There are also certain types of objects called objects of apprehension. There are different levels of objects.

Your Holiness, when you talk of subtle consciousness, is there a distinction between consciousness for itself, consciousness of something, and consciousness for something?

HH: It is very difficult to imagine consciousness without any object because the very term *consciousness* means to be conscious of something—an object. I think the term *consciousness* is applied to the gross level of the mind from the point of view of action. The subtle consciousness becomes obvious in ordinary persons only in an unconscious state—for example, in a faint.

When we consider the eight dissolution processes at death, the seventh is black, near attainment, which is divided into two: the first part still retains a subtle memory; and in the second part we lose that, also. We have this experience of Clear Light by the force of our own karmic actions. This is like a natural process of dissolution in which the aggregates we obtained as the consequence of our own karmic actions cease. We go through that process naturally.

There is a possibility of experiencing such a state of Clear Light through training in yoga, winds, and so forth, in which the meditator, by the force of his realizations, brings about this experience through meditation. Although at this point he experiences the subtle level of consciousness, he is conscious of it; he does not lose control. The meditator has to direct that type of experience to reality, the nature of emptiness. Does that answer your question?

Yes, thank you.

Are dreams significant? How do we interpret them, especially when they are truly wild?

HH: A certain dream may repeat itself again and again, and will be significant. The time of dreaming is also important. The dreams experienced at the time of dawn may be indications, so investigate the dreams seen around dawn. If one is very serious about this and wants to go further, dreams can be investigated with the assistance of certain yogas of wind. Through this practice, dreams become clearer and more definite. Generally, a dream is something that one takes to be illusive, without any truth.

According to Madhyamika Prasangika, the highest Buddhist school, all our experiences of consciousnesses, even during the waking state, are said to be mistaken in dependence on the appearance of the object. We misperceive them. Therefore, our experiences can be even more mistaken in dreams.

Under what condition will the dream-consciousness go outside of reality?

HH: When we are talking of dream-consciousness and the dream-body, we are talking about a very different kind of experience in which the body is autonomous, independent of the physical, gross body. We are on an entirely different plane. The dream-body can see actual reality. During the day, the dream-body of a person can see daytime: daytime is daytime; nighttime is nighttime.

The special dream-body can depart from this physical body. Many years ago I met a person who had that kind of experience—not due to practice but due to karma, experiences in past lives. That person felt very uncomfortable and asked me what to do. It seemed that during deep sleep that person went away and saw his friends, you see . . . he saw actual things, so that is the special dream-body.

Is meditation the only way to understand our sub-conscious, to tap into the power of dreams?

HH: The understanding of the nature of one's self has to develop through deep meditation—there is no other way. The subtler the level of consciousness is, the more profound the meditation becomes. The level of consciousness during the dream-state is subtler than that during the waking state. Meditation undertaken during the waking state is equal to the dream-state. Such methods are very powerful.

What I said earlier about investigating dreams is like this. Sometimes we have certain dreams that indicate that we are going to hear some sensational news the next day. We have the potential in our consciousness to foresee the future. Although we are not able to realize this potential fully, some indications can arise, but they are not always very reliable.

CHAPTER 11

SHUNYATA

Your Holiness, perhaps the most mystifying and fascinating concept of Buddhism is shunyata, *or emptiness. What is shunyata?*

HH: The meaning of *shunya* is not "nothingness," but the absence of an absolute essence. The Buddhist meaning of *shunyata* is the absence of independent existence or the objective side. The thing does exist, but that existence is due to other factors, not by itself.

When scientists were explaining quantum theory, they were reluctant to use the word *reality* as if it is independent. For many, *reality* means some independent reality of nature, but of course there is no such thing. The thing does not exist in itself; its existence is due to other factors—causes and conditions.

There is a similarity between this scientific finding and the Buddhist explanation—nonexistence by itself or absence of independent existence, and, therefore, there is impermanence or momentary change. At the atomic level and the subatomic level, things are always changing.

Is emptiness like a seed?

HH: It is not quite like that. Emptiness is not like being a seed, not like space as a basis for all the planets and stars—not that kind. Emptiness in the sense of shunyata is explained on the basis of something that exists that has a connection with reality. Any phenomenon has emptiness as its own nature; and any phenomenon is pervaded by its own nature, emptiness, which is the absence of its true existence.

Emptiness is a quality, the ultimate quality of things. For example, the phenomena that depend on causes have one quality of momentary change. Furthermore, how does momentary change become possible—through emptiness, through its own quality? When we say "quality," there must be some basis for quality. Without that basis, there is no quality.

It would then seem logical to argue that our own sensorial perception is fundamentally illusory and we must not take any of the information it gives us seriously. If we actually started behaving like that, life would become rather difficult.

HH: What we are concerned with here is something a little different. When we consider that the sensorial consciousness is mistaken, we are not looking down on it. The very purpose of our efforts to understand emptiness is to bring about the experience of more happiness through the sense-data rather than more suffering. The question is whether the sensorial consciousnesses are mistaken or not. We have to understand that one consciousness can be both mistaken and valid at the same time. That distinction has to come from the difference in the object.

We talk about the apparent object, the object of apprehension, and the object of reference. We talk about valid sensorial consciousness—for example, my eye-consciousness that sees a flower. As far as its approach to the object of apprehension—this flower—is concerned, it is not mistaken; it is valid. At the same time, that eye-consciousness has the appearance of the flower as truly existent, and from that point of view, it is mistaken.

Then would you clarify "truly existent"?

HH: One really has to think deeply about these things. It is not the kind of thing that can be explained by someone with knowledge and which the other person will immediately understand. It is not like pointing to a car and saying, "There is a car. . . . Oh! Yes! There is a car. Yes, yes, now I realize it is a car." Knowledge and one's own experience go together, and time is also involved. You cannot experience this within days or weeks; it can even take years of concentration—thinking and thinking about it—and then it becomes clearer and clearer.

When we try to interpret the meaning of "truly existent" in connection with emptiness, it does not mean it is true or false. Since the existence of phenomena is not dispelled by any valid cognition, they are truly existent. But because they do not exist the way they appear to our mistaken consciousness—because when we search for their essence, we do not find it—they are not inherently existent.

As I explained earlier, what is meant by "truly existent" is "inherent existence," something that is independent; these words themselves go 'round and 'round and 'round. . . .

The method employed to investigate reality may color your perception of reality. What you perceive is conditioned by what you are looking for: if you choose a logical method, you find A; if you take a direct perception, you might find B. Is this true or not?

HH: Yes, that is possible through your process of logic. But when we are concerned with establishing emptiness, we are trying to approach reality, the facts. We make the distinction between what is mere projection, the postulated view, and some partial views . . . and so on. The conclusion we are looking for is the realization of the fact—nature as it is—rather than trying to support a postulated stand.

The philosophical thought, for example, in Cittama-tra [the "Mind-Only" school], in which they distinguish between external object and subjective mind, is just a postulated view. It does not tally with actual reality.

Nagarjuna, in Madhyamika Mulakarika, clearly stated that "the appropriator and what is being appropriated should be different." Therefore, the self or the "I" is a mere designation. Without any investigation, we satisfy ourselves and say, "I am going," "I am hungry," "I am tired," "I am older." All this is said by people without investigation, because as soon as you go out to investigate, you will not be able to find it. That is a sign of the absence of an absolute.

Thus, as I said, the meaning of *shunya* is not "nothingness," but the absence of an absolute essence. Yes, it works, but collectively with many other factors. Without those factors, you cannot find it. You can't pinpoint it. Nothing . . . for that matter, even the Buddha himself . . . can be pinpointed. You can't say what Buddha is, apart from Buddha's physical body and his mind. So the ultimate meaning of selflessness is that there is no absolute essence. It is merely a designated self, which comes from the past life and goes to the next. But that designation is based on the combination of body and mind.

Again, there exist more subtle levels of body and mind. So, in this life, the human being is designated on the basis of his body and mind. But as soon as the body dissolves, there exists no self in physical terms, but a subtle self does exist. Buddha has said innumerable times that everything is a mere designation.

However, when we say that all phenomena are designated, it doesn't imply that whatever one designates can come into being. It doesn't happen that way. Even if you forcibly call an animal's body and mind a human being, it will not become one. So, that is contradictory. Therefore, designations should not contradict accepted norms and conventions.

Perhaps it would help to delve deeper into the meaning of dependent and independent existence.

HH: First of all, we have to distinguish between conventional and inherent existence. Let me first speak about the reasoning for dependent arising; that will give us the answer.

Dependent arising means interdependence. To understand it, one has to understand the theory that dependence and independence are directly opposite phenomena, which exclude the middle. There is nothing that is neither of the two.

For example, flower and nonflower are direct opposites. Any phenomenon should be either flower or nonflower; there is no third way of existence. On the other hand, let us consider a flower and a table. Although these are mutually exclusive, there is something that is neither of the two; there is a middle. In the same way, being independent and being dependent are directly opposite.

Those phenomena, which are products of causes, depend for their existence on their causes and conditions. In the same way, if it is a whole, it is very obvious that it is dependent on its parts. As long as the phenomenon retains its quality of form, it would always have its directional parts. Things that have no quality of form—for example, consciousness—do have parts of different instances, such as "earlier," "later," and so on.

Does a phenomenon that is partless exist? Physically, one can get down to the subatomic level, where there is hardly any possibility of a further division of particles. However, there would be directional parts; there is no partlessness. Would you say partlessness exists?

If subatomic particles were partless and had no directional parts, how could one say that the composite of such particles can produce a whole? If it is without directional parts, whatever faces the east should also face the west. So, in that case, there is no possibility of making composites from these sources, is there?

The writings of the Madhyamika school totally negate the theory of partless phenomena. The existence of each phenomenon depends on its own parts. These are the two ways of depending: on causes and conditions, and on parts.

Another type of dependence is that nothing is "findable" when we analytically search for its essence. If we are content with mere conventional appearance, everything is okay. But if we are not satisfied with mere conventional appearance and search for the essence, for some kind of justification for the object, we do not find anything. When we finally get to the point when we realize that we cannot find it through analysis, the question of whether that is an indication that things do not exist at all comes up.

If we had to say that things do not exist at all, our own experience would contradict it. Our experience shows that there is one person who did not find the essence and who found the "unfindable." This valid cognition that perceived the person who was seeking the essence and the "unfindability" of the thing would contradict the assertion that things do not exist at all. Therefore, there should be something there; things are there.

Yet, when we investigate, we cannot find them. The conclusion to be drawn is that things exist but on the basis of imputation. They depend on nominal designation. No matter how we look at things, they always show the characteristics of dependency. Being dependent on *causal factors,* on *parts,* or on *consciousness that assigns the designation* are the three types of dependence.

One must analyze what the actual nature is. How does the thing appear to us? Then we should check whether the way things appear and the way things actually exist correspond. Do they tally or not? We find that there is a gap between the way things appear and the way they actually exist.

Is there a process of analysis that can help me actually perceive shunyata?

HH: There are many things that we cannot come to conclusions about when we analyze them. We just have to leave them as they are, take them at their face value. If one goes into too much detail, things become absurd.

Take shunyata as one example. There is shunyata, and there is function; therefore, there must be some basis that allows this function. If we investigate what shunyata is, we can vaguely say that the absence of independent existence is shunyata. Then, when we look at it minutely, this shunyata, that shunyata, even shunyata as ultimate reality—when we follow this process and search for the essence of shunyata—we cannot find it. We find that shunyata depends very much on the ways in which it is qualified, the object on which it is qualified.

I had a very interesting discussion with scientists on the subjects of neurobiology and psychology. I feel that compared to Eastern psychology, Western psychology is very young. The means of investigation are different from ours.

From my experience, there are scientists who state they are radical materialists and do not even accept the existence of the mind. This has happened, but as

discussions ensue, scientists show more and more interest in the Buddhist explanations of the mind, matter,
atoms, phenomena, and the like. We derive benefit from
their research and findings, and the Buddhist interpreta-
tion gives them a different perspective through which to
investigate. That is my experience.

But despite a genuine desire to accept and understand the
essential emptiness of things, I struggle with my mind and its
concepts of "reality."

HH: When we experience a negative state of mind
through hatred or desire, it is caused by our concept of
something as being good or bad. Then, in turn, we find
that our concept of good or bad is polluted by a super-
imposed special goodness or repulsion of the object,
which, in turn, is caused by holding something as truly
good or truly bad. Buddhists say that all these negative
states of mind have their root in ignorance, which grasps
at the true existence of phenomena.

Let me give you an example: Let's look at the two
basic kinds of mind. One kind arises upon the confirmation of the appearance of true existence. The second
type of mind depends for arising upon the confirmation
of that kind of projected appearance, such as anger or
strong attachment. The moment we feel attachment and
anger, not only is there appearance but also some kind
of confirmation, and we accept that it is 100 percent
positive and feel attached or 100 percent negative and
feel angry.

But, factually, if we see an enemy as 100 percent
enemy, he should be everybody's enemy. But my enemy

might be the best friend of others. So when my enemy is 100 percent negative, there is some truth in it from that side—independent, not dependent on the side of the subject or projected mind.

But no enemy can be 100 percent negative. Therefore, it is an exaggeration—the result of my feeling of strong dislike. All negative thought must have that kind of confirmation. Positive thought is not necessarily based on that. And in order to minimize negative thought, the realization of shunyata is important.

Is there a conflict that arises, then, at a visible level when we negate all that we know and love as illusion and inherently empty?

HH: It is very important to see the difference between the way the nonconceptual mind, such as sensorial perception, approaches an object and how mental consciousness, which is mostly conceptual, approaches an object. One has to see the difference between the two.

The reasoning process that is employed in establishing emptiness should be such that it never harms the validity of sensorial experience . . . not harming in the sense that it should not prevent it, suppress it. When we talk about delusions, they are only on the mental level. Sensorial consciousnesses are never delusions; they are mistaken, but they are not afflicted emotions.

Second, there are the different types of mental apprehensions of the object, which qualify the object as inherently existent or not.

Third, when an object is apprehended without any such qualification, it is just an object.

There are three ways of experiencing the object. When the conceptual mind approaches an object, it does so by excluding something.

Therefore, the realization of emptiness counters the type of mental apprehension that perceives the object with the qualification as inherently existent, but it does not harm the type of consciousness that apprehends the object without any qualification (which can be the sensorial perception of the object).

Confusion exists regarding the term *true,* and this confusion arises even in the Tibetan language. Without much familiarization through logic or meditation, it is difficult to understand this. It is the same, for example, with the Sanskrit word *swabhava*—nature—which can mean different things according to different occasions and contexts at the conventional level and at the deeper level.

So when we say "true existence," the meaning of *true* is very mixed, unless we have some state of experience. Even I find it very difficult to explain.

Mind must investigate shunyata, and mind must have direct experience of it, too. Is there a contradiction, then, between subjective mind and objective mind? And which mind is experiencing emptiness when it is itself nonexistent?

HH: When we talk of the emptiness of true existence, we do not distinguish between object and subject, because both have no true existence. If we search, we cannot find the object or subject mind itself. Mind can be taken as an object of some other observing consciousness. In this relative context, it becomes the object. At that point, when we search for it, we will not find it just as the object. The ultimate reason for negating true existence is that it is unfindable when you search for its essence. That is the ultimate reason.

Scientists are generally skeptical about what they cannot definitely see. However, I believe that science itself has limitations. It is limited to the field that you can measure, that is measurable. Life, consciousness, minds—these have not yet been explored fully. They are definitely connected with the brain. Today scientists are investigating the relationship between the mind and the brain and will gain more knowledge about the nature of the mind and mental functions. There is interdependence—what we call *shunya,* or emptiness.

But what do we do with our feelings?

HH: There we are talking on the relative level. We just accept feeling and recognition—*this is a flower, this is a man, this is an Indian, this is a Tibetan*—without any investigation. No problem, this is the conventional level. Further questions: *Who am I? What is the being? What is the self?* That is the door or the stage . . . from that point of view, we cannot find it.

And consciousness within emptiness is . . . ?

HH: Yes, again consciousness, but what is consciousness? We feel consciousness. We have a feeling of cognition that we call consciousness—*today my mind is dull; today my mind is clear*—we can say that again without investigation, without penetration.

Then take one particular subject, for example, consciousness. What is consciousness? We cannot find it. Finger? Very easy. My finger? Here. Nobody argues. I actually see the color of my finger, its shape, and so on. So what is "finger"? Is it color or the substances: skin, blood, bone? If we analyze the particles, the parts of the finger, the different substances, we do not find the "finger."

When we analyze further, we find there are two levels: one is the relative or conventional level; the other is the deeper or ultimate level. There is someone here who cannot find the finger. There is such a person because he exists conventionally.

We do not make such distinctions because at the conventional level both of them exist; at the ultimate level neither exists.

One of the Buddhist schools says that the thing you are looking for does not exist, but the person who finds that there is nothing, he truly exists.

Your Holiness, is it possible to grasp dependent arising without the purification of delusions?

HH: One can realize dependent arising while still having delusions with the ordinary mind. Investigate shunyata on the basis of this relative theory and you can understand shunyata. Thinking about it intellectually and meditating on it, you can feel it.

But we have to distinguish between the consciousness that realizes the nature of dependent arising, or inferential understanding, and direct experience.

Ordinary beings can have inferential understanding of emptiness. In order to have direct experience, one has to decrease the force of delusions that we ordinary beings have. Realizing emptiness directly serves as further purification. You will find that the realization of emptiness is not so difficult.

Are there practices on shunyata that can help?

HH: Yes. I can say that quite a few people exist who have realized emptiness. My own experience, I don't know. About 15 or 20 years ago, I started to think very intently about shunyata. One can get some kind of deep understanding. But you see, in the Dalai Lama's case the problem is time.

Why is that?

HH: I cannot spend the whole time thinking, meditating. I have to divert my mind into many different activities. That is the problem.

CHAPTER 12

PHENOMENA

Your Holiness, at the entrance of your monastery in Dharamsala an inscription reads: "All existence is like a reflection, clear and pure without turbulence; it cannot be grasped and it cannot be expressed. Without self-nature, without location, perfectly established by way of their causes and actions." Would you please explain this inscription?

HH: It means that speaking from the viewpoint of ordinary consciousness like ours, all phenomena are like reflections. Although they appear in one way, they exist in another way. They appear as truly existent, but they do not exist truly. Therefore, there is a contradiction, just as a reflection of a face appears in a mirror as if it were the face itself, and yet it is not the face.

The second line says that it is clear and pure, without turbulence. There are two interpretations: one according to the sutra, and one according to tantra. This has to be explained according to the context in which it is quoted; and I shall give an explanation, as I understand it, as I remember it.

These three factors—being clear, pure, and without turbulence—refer to the three objects of abandonment: obscuration of delusions, obscuration to knowledge, and obscuration to absorption . . . the meditative state. This statement also refers to the pure nature of phenomena, emptiness; it has no stains, no impurities. To give an explanation of this line, in conjunction with the three types of abandonment, it says that by understanding the nature of non-inherent existence to the fullest extent, one is freed from the three types of obscuration.

The third line, "it cannot be grasped and it cannot be expressed," means that such an experience cannot be grasped by persons like ourselves through our conceptual thought, nor can it be expressed fully through conventional words.

The last line, "without self-nature, without location, perfectly established by way of their causes and actions," I think, refers to the three doors of liberation. It explains the emptiness of phenomena itself, its causes, and its effects.

According to the shunyata principle, truth begins by accepting the nonexistent nature of all phenomena. But then this "tangible" world of ours must have some kind of basis? What is its form, basis, and designation, which we ascribe to all that we call our world and you refer to as phenomena?

HH: Form is the designated phenomenon. It is a form, but its designated basis is not form. To give an example on the basis of the self, let us say that a person has all the five aggregates, such as form, feeling, and so on. This self is a designated phenomenon labeled on the basis of the collection of all the five aggregates. However, from within these five aggregates, we cannot find anything that could be said to be the person or the being. Separate from the whole and the parts of the aggregates, we cannot find the person either. Yet, it is not that the person does not exist at all. Where is the person, then?

There is a certain relationship between the basis of designation and the designated phenomenon. However, it is neither the relationship between cause and effect nor of generality and instances; it is a mere interdependent relationship.

This is one of the roots of the Madhyamika view, and the most important and difficult point. When we talk of the designated basis, the identification of the designated basis is a very difficult task. I think that since things do not truly exist, the only choice left for their mode of existence is their true convention. Although we make a difference between the object, the phenomena, and the subject, the mind—the subject mind—is also a phenomenon. From the viewpoint of one particular consciousness, there is the object phenomenon and the subject mind. But consciousness itself is also a phenomenon, because there is another subjective mind that takes it, which is an object, which realizes it.

The meaning of non-inherent existence is something like that. You give this label by dependence on a basis, which is not the phenomenon itself.

Your Holiness, the Madhyamika Prasangika states that phenomena exist merely by implication. If that is true, it refutes the external existence of the object. Isn't that liable to the fault of eternalism?

HH: When Madhyamika Prasangika speaks of phenomena existing as mere imputations, this "mere" does not refute external objects, the phenomena that are not names; and neither does it refute that phenomena are not perceived by valid cognition. Although there is a phenomenon that is not a name itself, it exists only through the power of convention. When Madhyamika Prasangika came to the conclusion that the essence of phenomena cannot be found when searched for analytically, this is not an indication of its nonexistence but rather an indication of its non-inherent existence.

It is not like finding nothing, but it *is* something, as explained in the opening verse of Mulamadhyamakakarika —"The Fundamental Wisdom of the Middle Way"—by Nagarjuna: that the examination of inherent existence should be made on a phenomenon that has the qualities of going and coming, production and cessation, and so forth on the conventional level. On the basis of such a phenomenon, we have to refute inherent existence. One can almost say that this table is non-inherent because it is existent; since it exists, it should exist dependently on other factors. The very fact of its existence proves its non-inherent existence.

On the other hand, when the Mind-Only school analytically search for the existence of external objects and dissect or analyze the parts of an object, they do not find the whole. Since they cannot posit the mere imputation existing by the power of imputation alone, they say there is no external object apart from consciousness. They say that external objects do not exist as separate entities from the consciousness.

I don't know myself. It is not very clear right from the beginning. When they analytically search for an external object by dissecting it into parts and cannot find it, the question arises if such things as form and so on exist. Their answer is that there is an object, but it is not a different substance from the consciousness. It is of the same substance as consciousness. Therefore, there are no external objects. Internal consciousness, therefore, is truly existent, is independent.

Samkhya, a non-Buddhist school of philosophy, asserts that phenomena are naturally permanent but temporarily impermanent. They have a different viewpoint. This needs clarification.

HH: If we have to detach from things simply because they are impermanent, we should detach from the path we are seeking because it is impermanent. The question is not whether it is impermanent or permanent. The question is whether it is worthwhile to feel desire for it or not, worthwhile to achieve. If yes, there is the desire to get. I think we can make this distinction and detach.

Within desire, there is proper desire and improper desire. Proper desire is when we find, through investigation and reasoning, that its fulfillment is worthwhile. In such a case, wish or attachment can be correct—for example, the desire to achieve Buddhahood or the desire to work for the benefit of all sentient beings. These we should deliberately try to develop in our minds. We should make special efforts to develop the feeling that all sentient beings are "mine."

In the case of an improper desire, you want something, but when you think about it more deeply, you find you do not really need it. For example, when you go to a supermarket, there are plenty of good things there, and you want them all. You count your money, and the second thought that comes to your mind is: do you really need all that? And you answer, *Oh! It's not necessary!*

This is my own experience. Such desire is really attachment or greed. In order to live comfortably, to survive, these things are not really necessary.

For a layman, family life is normal, but when it is explained in relation to cultivating a path to achieve liberation, the important thing is not to fall under the sway of delusions. This is rather difficult. Now, if a good practitioner remains a monk or nun, under certain circumstances people may feel that here is an exceptional person, but with less influence—less useful to society as a whole.

So be a good practitioner, but also remain a good member of society, a productive person. Remain with your family; earn a livelihood; be a good, honorable person with inner peace; and create a peaceful atmosphere within your own family, which helps to create a peaceful atmosphere within the community. Such a person with bodhicitta, altruism, can be more useful to society as a layperson with a family life.

However, if one wants to achieve the path chiefly for one's own concern or benefit, then the life of a celibate is recommended. Sometimes even leading a family life is recommended. In the sutras, we find many bodhisattvas who led family lives, but we hardly find mention of arhats leading family lives.

*Are you then saying that the phenomenon, as we under-
stand it, is the designation, even though it arises in dependence on the cause and yet is not the cause, but purely a
mental construction?*

HH: Although phenomena are imputed by conceptual thought, anything cannot exist just by labeling. It is
not that anything that is imputed by a consciousness can
become it. It cannot be manipulated as the consciousness wishes it. If consciousness or conceptual thought
could do what it wanted, there would be no difference
between valid and invalid cognition or right and wrong.
No difference would ever arise. Since phenomena do
exist and their true existence has been refuted logically,
the only choice left—whether we like it or not—is that
they exist nominally, through designation. But this does
not mean that anything we designate would *become* it.

*Phenomenon is not the basis—that is my question. Is
there a distinction between the basis and the phenomenon?*

HH: This requires an explanation of the three factors: the base of designation, the conceptual thought
that gives the label, and the actual designated phenomenon. When a consciousness searches for the designated
phenomenon within or from the basis, it does not find
any example that can be posited as the phenomenon.
The base of designation is not the designated phenomenon. But neither do we give the label to a thing that is
not it; otherwise we could call an elephant a horse and
so forth. The designation is not given to a phenomenon
that is not it.

As we cannot give the label to a thing that is not the phenomenon itself, and as we also cannot find an example within the designated basis that can be said to *be* the phenomenon, the choice left is to give the designation in dependence on the basis. If there is no phenomenon, the convention is contradicted. There is something on the conventional level, and the thing we get at the end is the mere designation.

But in understanding the nature of reality, at one level I feel, and you reiterate this, that everything is one. Yet when we talk about phenomena and perception, we talk about it as if it were two, three, four, or five different things.

HH: The Two Truths are an explanation of one object looked at from two different angles. Since the Two Truths are explained on the basis of one object, they are actually of one entity, but they are also regarded as mutually exclusive.

Let us take the example of a person who is very learned, a very able person, but also very cunning. We want to employ that person for his ability, but that person is not trustworthy. From that angle, we have to take other measures, be careful. Although we deal with the same person, there is a contradiction; there are two aspects: one very negative, the other very positive.

If we consider this flower . . . it has a relative level of existence where all the conventions operate, such as color, scent, and so on. And then there is the deeper, ultimate reality. This is like looking at one object from two sides. Because of phenomena being dependently arising, they lack inherent existence, also called true existence.

Since they originate dependently, they are also deeply interconnected; even the understanding of the two is interconnected.

Some texts say that, at the ordinary level, sentient beings do have different entities, that they are different beings. Ultimately, when they become enlightened, they all become one, absorbed into one wisdom-ocean. Water coming from different rivers has different colors, tastes, speed . . . but when it merges with the infinite ocean, it loses its identity and becomes of one taste, the same color, and so on.

This does not mean that when a person reaches Buddhahood, his own personal identity is no more; it is not like that. He reaches the same kind of rank, and he is completely the same as the others at that level, yet the individual self or "I" is still there.

We have gotten ourselves into a lot of trouble by making various distinctions between black and white, either/or, and making objections to this or that. We are looking at the world as if it seems to be more complicated, and allows for more contradictions and paradoxes, and affirms the end of relative experience and ultimate experience. It does not seem so exclusive.

But then even within phenomena, there are negative phenomena and positive phenomena? What is the difference?

HH: When Buddhists talk about emptiness, emptiness is a negative phenomenon, and verses are positive phenomena. That does not mean that emptiness is nonexistent, but rather that it is the mere absence of inherent existence. It is the same when we talk of space.

The Buddhist concept of space is the mere absence of an obstruction, of form. This does not mean that there is no space, but that we cannot approach it.

To understand this is very difficult. It can only be completely understood by someone who has experienced shunyata, who has negated the misconceived nature of phenomena, who has negated inherent existence. The way in which phenomena exist through mere designation can only be understood through the experience of emptiness. For us ordinary people, the appearance of phenomena themselves and the appearance of their true existence are very mixed. We cannot really discriminate between the two: the actual appearance of the object and the true existence of the object.

One can also reflect here on what the Yogacarins [adherents of the Yogacara school] mean by saying that all phenomena are mere projections of the mind and when the Madhyamika school says that all phenomena are mere imputations by the mind. It is worth looking for the difference between the two. One has to take into account the context in which the statement was made.

Your Holiness, is logic the ultimate value?

HH: Logic should be something that can be traced to direct experience. However, there are different types of phenomena. Our level of intelligence can approach some types of phenomena. There are other types of phenomena that we are not able to perceive or approach unless our states of mind are heightened. Even such higher states adhere to the law of logic.

In Mahayana Buddhism, one clear implication is that there are two types of teachings: definitive and interpretive. Some of the Buddha's teachings can be taken at their face value, literally. Others cannot be taken literally. How do we determine what can be taken literally or not? This can be determined only through logical reasoning, because the definitive and interpretive meanings of the words are explained differently in the texts themselves.

If we had to determine whether the words in one of Lord Buddha's scriptures are definitive or interpretive, we would have to consult another scripture, and this could go on indefinitely. If the Buddha were alive today, we could ask him to tell us the definitive points. To avoid endless arguments, we decide, finally, through logical reasoning.

It is said that a scholar or person who adheres to a position that is contradictory to logical reasoning is not an authentic or valid scholar or person. For obvious reasons, we make a distinction between the intention of the scripture and the intention of the actual speaker. Since we have to get to the point of understanding the actual intention of the Buddha through logical reasoning, the position that cannot be contradicted by reasoning is the ultimate viewpoint of the Buddha.

Are the desire for permanence, the ego, and selfishness the primary delusory states that are targeted by the teachings of phenomena and shunyata?

HH: The question that arises is whether the mind can be freed from those delusions. One reason is that all negative states of mind have their root in the self-grasping attitude, grasping at true existence. This is a mistaken consciousness that can be shown as distorted. By refuting grasping at true existence, one can cut the roots of all these delusions. Another reason is, as we discussed before, the Buddha nature, the potential within ourselves to achieve Buddhahood.

Through these two types of reasoning, one has to prove the possibility that the mind can be freed from delusions. First, one must understand that the wisdom realizing emptiness, the wisdom realizing selflessness, and the consciousness that grasps at true existence are antidotes to each other. There also exists the difference of one having valid support and the other lacking valid support.

The wisdom realizing selflessness is a quality of the mind and not of the body. It has long-lasting continuity. Any quality that is based on the body is something temporary. A quality that is based on the mind, or consciousness, is sounder, since the continuity of the mind, the quality, is always there. The quality has a very firm basis, and once fully experienced, it does not require reassertion for its increase; it has the quality of infinite increase. On the other hand, an attitude that grasps at true existence is a consciousness that has a very powerful antidote, and once we develop familiarity with that antidote, it can be lessened and finally purged.

If so, how does the theory of understanding phenomena as basically nonexistent help in our spiritual evolution?

HH: Misbehavior of the body and speech are the manifestations of these delusions. Later, during the second stage, one must work toward prevention of these delusions themselves. During the third stage, one must work toward the elimination of imprints left by these delusions. Through these three stages, we achieve the following results:

- **First**, the result of refraining from misbehavior of body and speech is that we have taken rebirth in a higher state as human beings.

- The result of the **second** stage, the abandonment of all delusions, is the achievement of nirvana or liberation.

- And **third**, the state in which we abandon even the imprints left behind by delusions is called the omniscient state.

When, on the basis of the pure phenomenon, which is the non-inherent nature of the mind, one has completely abandoned all delusions, one has reached the state of cessation.

Thinking along these lines, one comes to realize that there is such a thing, cessation in general, and also that it is possible that it materializes in one's own mind. Since it is natural for us not to desire suffering, and when we find that there is a possibility to free ourselves from suffering, we have to work for the achievement of such a state. For this reason, the path is explained.

Therefore, Buddhism says that unless one has achieved wisdom realizing selflessness, one cannot have the experience of moksha.

CHAPTER 13

THE POWER OF MEDITATION AND VISUALIZATION

Your Holiness, what is meditation?

HH: Meditation, from the Buddhist viewpoint, is something like an instrument to channel our minds and to increase our mental capacity. It means *samadhi*—that is, channeling our mental energy. Meditation is an instrument to increase our mental energy and mental sharpness, or alertness.

Can meditation be secular, or does it have to follow a particular religious tradition?

HH: No, no! It is simply a training of the mind.

Is there any relationship between meditation and religion?

HH: Meditation is the instrument to shape or transform the mind. Whether you are a businessman, scientist, doctor, or teacher, if your mind is more alert, more calm, and sharp, it's very useful for you. The mind is a prime mover, so the training of the mind is very useful in all fields. So meditation is essentially not a religious subject.

In fact, all of the world's major religions carry the same message of compassion, love, forgiveness, and spirit of harmony. However, this does not mean that if you accept these values, you must accept religion as a whole. We have to make a distinction between purely religious subjects, such as faith, and basic good qualities. These are two things.

To me, I think all major religions simply strengthen the basic good qualities, nothing else. So long as we are human beings, and we want to be happy human beings and live in happy human societies, there is no point in neglecting these basic good human qualities. Clearly, without them the individual or the family or the community will not be happy.

How is meditation linked to achieving happiness?

HH: I have always believed that the very purpose of our lives is happiness. There are two kinds of happiness—one comes from physical comfort, and the other is at the mental level or through mental training.

Obviously, between the two, mental comfort is superior and more influential because if our mental state is calm and happy, small physical discomforts—even small pains—can be subdued. On the other hand, if our mind is restless, we will not be happy even with the best facilities. That's very clear. Therefore, the mental experience is more important than the physical one.

Of course, experience implies some kind of feeling, feeling of the mind. The immediate cause is physical, and the other is mainly the mind itself, so there are two kinds of experiences. Since mental experience is very important, it automatically brings up another subject —can we train ourselves to develop it? Humankind, on an average, is quite smart, not like other species, because only human beings have invented techniques to shape their minds. These techniques we usually call meditation.

Are there different kinds of meditation? Why is it important in our daily lives?

HH: Broadly, there are two kinds of meditation. One is analytical, mainly utilizing reason; the other is where the mind stays still on a single point without change or investigation—"single-pointedness." In both cases, the main purpose is that our minds come to draw the point that we want to reach.

For example, mental attitude is so influential in daily life that when you wake up in the morning and your mind feels happy or fresh, the rest of the day is good even in the face of a problem. If your mood is dull, even small things may lead you to eventually "burst." So, you see, mental attitude is a very important factor in our daily lives.

How much importance should one give to the place of meditation?

HH: For a beginner, the place of meditation is quite important. Once we have developed some experience, external factors have very little effect. For people who have a chance to stay in remote places, there is no problem. But whether we like it or not, we have to remain in our places: you in Delhi, me in Dharamsala. These are our fixed places.

The place for meditation should ideally be quiet. And when we meditate on single-pointedness of mind, we need a completely isolated place—no noise. This is very important. For certain yoga practices, the altitude also makes a difference. A higher altitude is better, so high mountains are the best place.

There is also another factor: places where experienced meditators have lived earlier have been blessed and charged by them. Later, persons of less experience receive the vibrations or blessings from it and get charged by the place.

Your Holiness, you speak of two kinds of meditation, and both train the mind. How do we decide which one is most suitable for us?

HH: Now, how do we train our minds? As I mentioned before, there are two methods. One is analytical meditation; and that, I feel, is more effective because of human intelligence or discriminative awareness. (My English vocabulary is poor, and my understanding of meanings is very limited, so sometimes I may use the wrong terms.) As a result of human intelligence or discriminative awareness, we have a tendency to know more: the "unless-you-can-see-the-reason-you-can't-accept" attitude is very healthy. From the Buddhist viewpoint, a skeptical attitude is appropriate—that is, not to easily accept, but to wait and carry out experiments and look for reasons.

Once you see the reason and through experiment gain experience, you accept it—that's the Buddhist attitude and a scientific approach. Using reason is essential so that concepts can be challenged.

With analytical meditation, you analyze the situation using reason and experiments, and develop genuine conviction. Once conviction is developed, your belief or faith is firm. Even if someone questions you, you will have experimented and analyzed the situation and will remain firm in your convictions.

With single-pointed meditation, you simply meditate on a point, not necessarily to develop some kind of firm conviction. If contradictory evidence is placed before you, you may immediately change your mind. Analytical meditation, thus, is much more effective and important.

In both cases, when you analyze a situation, your mind should channel all your mental energy so that the analysis becomes much more forceful and goes deeper. For that, too, we need some kind of single-pointedness. Perhaps, if you have some experience of single-pointed meditation, it enhances and betters the quality of your analytical meditation.

Please elaborate on the technique of single-pointedness. Some people close their eyes, and others don't. Which is the right method?

HH: Usually, it is best to try this in a place with less noise—the noise of airplanes; cars, trucks, and honking; wind; or waterfalls. But we have to utilize our own place as effectively as possible. So the best time is early in the morning when truck drivers are sleeping! There is comparatively less noise, and most important, our minds are fresh.

Mental training means shaping our minds. This is done through the mind itself, and not by external means. The mind must be very fresh and fully alert, with no feeling of tiredness. If you utilize that kind of mental state, it can work most effectively. Late evening, our mind is dull, and there is a feeling of tiredness.

I think a simple start for a beginner is just to try to withdraw. The mind is always with the body and is not external to it. But our minds usually look outside, and that's a pity. We have to give a new instruction to our minds.

Up to now, you have checked the outside thoroughly. Now, the time has come to check the mind itself, so go inside. Sometimes if your eyes are closed, it is more helpful. In the long run, however, it does not matter whether your eyes are open or shut.

Visualize something inside and concentrate on it with your main mind. First, withdraw your mind, including sense of sight, sense of hearing, and so on. In the beginning, make the decision that for the next few moments, you will not let these sensory organs be distracted by external objects, and even if the senses go, your main mind will not follow.

Also, within the mind, you need to control thought. You should deliberately try to stop thoughts from the past and about the future. If you can sustain some kind of thoughtlessness a little bit longer, then eventually increase the duration. At that moment you may get a feeling of emptiness, nothingness, like space, or like a deep ocean where waves on the surface come and go, come and go, but the water itself is pure and clean. That's one way to look at the mind itself.

Although it is not easy, it's worthwhile to meditate, to try.

What does it mean to meditate on compassion?

HH: Genuine compassion is not a feeling of closeness as is generally known: *This is my close friend* or *This is good for me*—that is attachment, where much depends on the object. Such a mental attitude or feeling of closeness changes if the person changes slightly. Such a feeling cannot be developed for your enemy or unknown people.

Genuine compassion is mainly based on the realization that other human beings are just like me; they, too, want happiness; they also have the right to overcome suffering. On that basis there is a spirit of concern, a feeling of closeness. This is genuine compassion, and such compassion can be directed to your enemy. The "enemy" may be a person or a community that creates problems for us, that brings us harm.

But there is a way to see that very person or community from another angle—just like the way we see ourselves. They also have the right to overcome suffering.

On that basis we can develop genuine feelings of concern, genuine compassion.

To meditate on compassion, think of some unfortunate people, like those facing starvation or those with mental defects. If you keep them in mind, you will develop concern and compassion, and a kind of emotion that is based on reason. It is different from the attachment emotion. It is also different from the emotion of anger, which is basic nature and a kind of spontaneous emotional feeling. Genuine compassion cannot come spontaneously. It arises through analysis, reasoning, and thought; and is based on reason.

When you develop a strong feeling of compassion, meditate on it with your whole mind. Enter into it—and without thinking, without any disturbance; just simply meditate on it. Analyze it, finally sealing your mind, determined that you will remain on it. When you next feel weakened by something, again analyze it and try to develop a strong feeling, and then meditate on it. That's one way.

With days, weeks, and months, your mental attitude will eventually change. As compassion develops, it is easier to tackle anger, hatred, or negative emotions that are all very forceful. If you analyze it, there is no sound basis for these emotions, but at the moment they are very strong and difficult to control.

While training for compassion, and when you develop a feeling of appreciation for compassion, you will see the negativity of hatred and how it harms your health. When anger constantly comes and goes, there are blood-pressure problems, loss of sleep and appetite, and related problems. You may even quarrel with your dearest friend.

Whether at the international or national levels—family or individual levels—anger, I think, brings disaster. Sometimes it brings powerful, forceful energy, but that energy is blind, so one cannot be sure whether it is destructive or constructive.

Your Holiness, there is a popular drug in the West called Prozac, used to change the biochemistry in the brain so that one can feel happier. What would your response be to this technique in the pursuit of happiness?

HH: First of all, I am completely ignorant about this drug. I have no experience of it. My opinion is that the kind of happiness that you get from these drugs is actually a kind of hallucination—like too much alcohol. At certain times, you lose genuine sensory control.

You see, in our lives, there is always some kind of problem, and much depends on your mental attitude. But if due to some chemical, you feel, *Oh, everything is okay,* that's an illusion. I have often said that our basic problem is of being confined within ignorance, and, therefore, we are covered in a thick wall of illusion. We do not need additional illusions. I feel it is better to be realistic.

Can you tell us about vipasyana as a meditating technique?

HH: Vipasyana, according to the Indian master Asanga, is a kind of state in which we achieve mental subtleness after having employed analysis while retaining

155

the stability of concentration. The mind becomes more serviceable. That state of mind is known as *vipasyana*.

There are two major types of vipasyana: one that is focused on conventional phenomena, and one that is focused on emptiness. In vipasyana that is focused on conventional phenomena, one way is to concentrate on the breathing process. Vipasyana can also be practiced by visualizing deities or divine beings emanating from ourselves and absorbing them again. And then there is the third type, the worldly vipasyana practice, called comparative vipasyana, in which we focus on the faults of the desire realm and the advantages of the form and formless realms, higher realms.

Can vipasyana help us meditate on and understand emptiness? How does that happen?

HH: I shall explain briefly the meditation on emptiness within the reasoning of the absence of singularity and plurality. First of all, in order to meditate on emptiness, we have to identify the thing, the emptiness of which we are meditating on—that is, the thing to be negated. Unless we identify the object of negation, we cannot have the image of its absence. Therefore, first of all we must develop an understanding and an image of what is to be negated. For this, it is more convenient first to reflect on one's own self.

When we say, "I go," or "I eat," or "I stay," contemplate what kind of self or "I" appears to your mind. Try to recollect unpleasant situations in which you were unjustly blamed for something . . . or pleasant situations in which you were praised, very popular, and so forth.

During such experiences, you have a very fluctuating state of mind. At that time, you can identify that "I," or self, more clearly. Just think, when this "I" appears to your mind, does it appear as something separate from your body and mind? Like an independent entity? The type of "I" or self that appears to you so vividly that you feel you could put your finger on it, something independent from your own body and mind . . . that type of "I" is the most misconceived projection, and that is the object of negation. This is the first essential point—identifying what is to be negated.

If such an "I" or independent self exists, does it exist as one with the body and mind or truly separate from them, or is there is a third way in which it can exist? You have to look at the different possibilities. You will find that if it truly existed as an independent entity, it should be either one with the body and mind—the aggregates—or it should be separate, because there is no third way of existence. That is the second essential point.

The choices are that it is either one with the aggregates or totally different from them. If it is one with the aggregates, then just as the self is one, body and mind should be one, because they are identified with the self. If the self is separate, then just as the aggregates are manifold, in the same way the self should be manifold. If this independent self or "I" existed as something distinctly separate, truly apart from the aggregates, it should be findable even after the aggregates ceased to exist. This is not the case.

For example, at dawn or dusk when there is not much light, a coiled rope might look like a snake and frighten someone. Apart from the image of the snake in the mind of that person, there is no sense of true existence of a snake on the part of the object, the rope. In the same way, taking the aggregates, when you have the appearance of self on them, although such an appearance arises *from* the aggregates, there is not the slightest particle that can be identified as the self *within* the aggregates.

Just as the snake is only a misconceived projection and there is no true existence of the snake, in the same way, there is no true existence of the person; there is only a label imputed on the aggregates. As long as there is no essence existing on the part of the object concerned, in both cases they are the same.

In the Madhyamika system, the fundamental existence of things is taken to impute their fundamental emptiness. Is there a way of direct perception of this nonexistence for those of us who have not gained it through vipasyana?

HH: In order to develop the wisdom of perceiving emptiness or realizing emptiness, it is not necessary to achieve vipasyana or samatha. However, in order to make the wisdom realizing emptiness more powerful, and for further development, one requires vipasyana and samatha.

What you said is very correct. Things that exist conventionally can be affected by conventional functions; if there were such a case, one could, on the basis of that, explain emptiness. Since it lacks fundamental existence, it is possible to have all these seemingly different levels. What do you mean by the perception of emptiness? Do you mean not relying on reasoning?

Yes, I meant that if something is true, it should also tally with our own experience. That would be its test.

HH: Actual experience of emptiness at the initial stage—the fresh realization of emptiness—has to come from a logical process. It is not necessary to go into formalized reasoning as explained, but one has to apply reasoning and first gain inferential understanding, which can later lead to direct experience.

Vipasyana establishes impermanence in our minds and is a step toward selflessness, while tantric meditation through external form could be a distraction. I do not understand how this fits in with the simplicity of arriving at selflessness. Isn't vipasyana a simpler path than tantric meditation?

HH: Tantric meditation is difficult to practice; it is not at all easy. This is the special significance of tantric practice, the special meaning, special purpose: one mind practices two virtues simultaneously.

When in Sutrayana [as opposed to Tantrayana], the mind concentrates on shunyata, and we accumulate one kind of virtue. In that state, we accumulate stores of wisdom, but during that state one cannot accumulate stores of merit. At other times, when we practice the development of bodhicitta or compassion, *maitri,* we accumulate the other type of virtue: merit. During these moments, wisdom cannot develop.

In tantric practice, the wisdom that understands shunyata, that wisdom itself transforms into deities, mandalas, appearances, as a deity penetrates into the ultimate nature of the deity, shunyata. That wisdom creates both virtues simultaneously. Its explanation is quite easy, but its practice is very difficult! This tantric practice should also be categorized as vipasyana practice because there are many levels of vipasyana practice.

In Tibetan Buddhism, visualizing the female deity Tara and others as attributes of Buddha is considered an important technique. Please explain.

HH: The explanation in tantric practice is that there are different kinds of activities in which one can engage in relation to the different aspects of the Buddha's attributes and embodiment of different forms.

For the path, it is actually not necessary to visualize the Buddha. Without any visualization, simply meditate on shunyata, on the wisdom side; and bodhicitta, or altruism, on the method side, or *upaya*. But for tantric practice, it is usually necessary to practice visualizations, because the resultant state is one that has both the Form-body *(Rupakaya)* and the Truth-body *(Dharmakaya)*.

The main reason why we want to achieve Buddha-hood is to help other sentient beings. Also, the actual Buddha's quality, which helps and serves all sentient beings, is the Rupakaya, not the Dharmakaya. So when bodhisattvas cultivate a genuine aspiration to achieve enlightenment, they concentrate mainly on achieving the Form-body.

To achieve this, one has to accumulate the necessary causes and conditions. And this law of cause and effect pervades all impermanent phenomena, including the Buddha state. Therefore, one has to gather a substantial cause (karma) for this Form-body, but the practice of wisdom cannot become this substantial karma because the main function of accumulation of merit is the achievement of the Form-body. Form-body is like the resultant imprint of merit.

On the other hand, wisdom realizing emptiness is like a substantial karma for the achievement of the Truth-body. Since there are two types of resultant bodies, there are also two different causes. Although the practice of giving, morality, and the like can also be the cause for the Form-body, it cannot be the substantial cause for the Form-body. If that were the case, it would contradict the natural law of cause and effect.

The factor that serves as the complete, substantial cause for the Form-body is the one practice in tantra—the special energy, the winds. If this type of special energy is not generated with wisdom, there cannot be a combination of method and wisdom. Therefore, one should develop a mind that although of one entity, also has the part of wisdom and the part of method for the actualization of the Form-body and the Truth-body, complete within the entity of one mind.

Generally, if we ask what the Form-body looks like, there is no definite answer; one cannot say that it looks like a statue and so forth. But one can at least have an idea of something that can be imagined by humans. One should take the object of such a form or the image of a deity—which has similar features of the resultant Form-body—and focusing on such a form, reflect on its emptiness.

We then have the appearance of the deity and at the same time an understanding of its empty nature. Therefore, such a mind has both these qualities—the visualization of the deity and also the understanding of

161

emptiness—complete in it. For this reason it is necessary to visualize deities and mandalas in tantric practice.

Since we are meditating on deities, a part of mantra recitation of the particular deity is also included, but the actual practices should be done through mental meditation. However, when one feels tired at the end of the meditation session, instead of giving more work to the mind, one can give work to the mouth and repeat the mantras.

Do these deities represent different attributes of the Buddha?

HH: Yes. When we talk of these different aspects of the deities, there are two types of understanding. One is that these deities are different aspects of the different qualities of the Buddha. The other one arises when individuals take specific forms of the Buddha as their main meditational deity, and they meditate and practice on that basis. When they become enlightened, they becomes that deity. In that case, Tara, Avalokiteshvara, or Manjushri are different beings from Buddha Shakyamuni. At the same time, there are deities that are manifestations of one Buddha.

Your Holiness, how does one arrange the Objects of Refuge?

HH: The way in which different Objects of Refuge are to be arranged is also explained. If you can afford to have all the required religious objects, display them; but if you cannot, it does not matter that much.

The great meditator of Tibet, Yogi Milarepa, had nothing apart from new rolls of paper that contained instructions from his master Marpa, which he had put up around the cave. Although he did not have anything, a thief broke in one night. Milarepa laughed and said, "Since I cannot find anything here during the day, what is there that you can find at night?" It is said that a real meditator never feels the lack of external materials.

So are you saying that the motivation of the meditator is the most important ingredient?

HH: Yes. There is a story about one of the great meditators in Tibet. One day he arranged his offerings particularly well and then sat down and thought, *Why did I do that?* He realized that he had done it because he wanted to impress one of his benefactors who was coming to see him that day. He was so disgusted with his polluted motivation that he took a handful of dust and threw it over the offerings.

Another meditator was once a thief. Once when he visited a family, his right hand automatically reached out for a beautiful object. So, he caught his right hand with his left hand and called out, "There is a thief . . . there is a thief!"

This is really a very effective way of practicing because every moment the right thing is implemented. When we sweep, clean, or make some preparations, our motivation must be pure and sincere; our wish should not be to merely have a clean place, but also to put our mind in order. Worldly concerns must not be involved— or should be as little as possible.

Later, when we visualize the deities, make offerings, and recite mantras, it is as if preparations have been made to receive important guests. When we expect a guest, we first clean and tidy up, don't we? In order to practice meditation, first clean your room. Your wish to do so should not be polluted by negative states of mind such as attachment, hatred, or similar attitudes.

Your Holiness, in visualizing a deity, how is the choice made, and why?

HH: First, the statue of the Buddha needs to be explained. The Sanskrit term *Buddha* has a deep meaning. It means that one's mind is purified of faults and one's realizations have completely developed.

The Buddha is also known as Tathagatha, the one who has entered the nature of suchness and the one who arose from nature. When one explains the meaning of someone arising from nature, one comes to the three bodies of the Buddha: *Dharmakaya,* or Truth-body; *Sambhogakaya,* or Enjoyment-body; and *Nirmanakaya,* or Emanation-body. Detailed explanations of the three bodies of the Buddha can be found in Mahayana literature.

When the Buddha came into this universe as Buddha Shakyamuni, he assumed the Emanation-body from the Truth-body. All the great events in his life, starting from conception in the womb to his Parinirvana, are regarded as deeds of the Buddha; it is, therefore, believed that Buddha Shakyamuni is alive at this time, also.

The Buddha is also known as Sugatha—one who has passed into peace or the one who has traveled the peaceful path into a peaceful state. It also explains peaceful realizations, peaceful abandonment, or cessation. The

Buddha nature, which is inherent in all sentient beings, is also known as Sugatha, the essence of Buddha.

The body, speech, and mind of the Buddha are explained in different manifestations: the body as Avalokiteshvara, speech as Manjushri, and mind as Vajrapani. But in the text, Avalokiteshvara, Manjushri, and Vajrapani are explained as the embodiment of compassion, wisdom, and energy or right action of the Buddha. Avalokiteshvara, Manjushri, and Tara are peaceful deities; whereas Vajrapani is a slightly wrathful deity.

When someone has strong anger and force of mind, he can engage more forcefully in actions, and this is the reason for having wrathful deities. According to the highest Yogatantra, one calls this taking desire or hatred into the path. Tara is also spoken of as a purifying aspect of the body-winds, or the energy. All the different qualities of the Buddha—such as compassion, wisdom, power, and so on—depend on the moving factor, which is energy or mind, *prana*. One can also say that Tara is the feminine deity. According to a legend, Tara made it a point to become enlightened in her female form when she cultivated the aspiration to achieve enlightenment.

Your Holiness, would you please guide us through an actual meditative visualization?

HH: In the space before us, about four feet in front at the level of our eyes, the Objects of Refuge should be visualized in the nature of light. If we visualize the deities as bright rays of light, it will help eliminate mental sinking or sleepiness. On the other hand, if we visualize the deities as something heavy, solid, it will help us reduce mental excitement, which otherwise might disturb us.

To the right of the Buddha, visualize Bodhisattva Avalokiteshvara, white in color, which signifies purity. Manjushri, the embodiment of increasing wisdom, to the Buddha's left, is yellow. Yellow signifies increase. The unique feature of meditating on Avalokiteshvara is that it will increase the force of compassion, and meditating on Manjushri will increase wisdom.

Then we visualize Vajrapani in front of the Buddha—Vajrapani has slightly wrathful features. If you have indications of mysterious or invisible obstacles, then the recitation of the mantra of Vajrapani will help overcome them. Next, visualize Arya Tara behind the Buddha; the practice for longevity is mainly done through the meditation of Tara.

One recommendation on how to visualize all sentient beings is that on our right, we visualize all our male relatives, starting from our father; and on our left, all the female relatives, starting from our mother. Behind us are all the other sentient beings except our enemies, who are in front of us. We visualize these different sentient beings in the aspect of human beings who are, however, actively undergoing the sufferings of their different rebirths.

Reflect on the fact that just as we strongly desire happiness and want to avoid suffering, so do all sentient beings. Particularly those whom we fight as our enemies or suspect of wishing to harm us, people who irritate us—deliberately visualize these people in front of you and think, *Their nature as sentient beings is just like mine; they also want happiness, not suffering.*

If we develop a negative attitude, negative feelings, it won't harm *them,* will it? You will only lose your own peace of mind. Negative feelings might be worthwhile only if they hurt the others!

For that reason, the enemy is deliberately visualized in front—not out of some suspicious vigilance but just so as to practice in a more positive manner. Then, with deep sincerity, we recite these sacred words 21 times or as many times as we can:

> Namo Buddhaya
> Namo Dharmaya
> Namo Sanghaya

If you have the wish, the time, and if you feel the value of it, you can do the following practice. While you recite the Refuge formula with a certain motivation, a compassionate mind, and faith, you visualize the light rays emanating from the Objects of Refuge and entering your body and those of the sentient beings around you. Visualize that all negative attitudes, such as hatred, desire, ignorance, anger, and the like—within yourself and other sentient beings—are being pacified by these light rays.

Why is Tara used specifically for illness and long life, and how is it that you try to visualize rays of light when you are using her?

HH: There are many related texts of Tara that deal with the accomplishment of different activities. Just as Avalokiteshvara is seen as the embodiment of compassion and Manjushri of wisdom, Tara is seen as the embodiment of wind, prana. For the longevity of a person's life, the continuity of the inner winds is very important. I think there is a link between these two, because there are some practices for the prolongation of life in which one holds the breath.

When we engage in the visualization of the practice, we visualize the mantra circle at the heart of Tara. Light rays emanate from that circle and dissolve into our body generally, but particularly at the points where we have pain. The light rays are hot or cold, depending on the type of illness we are suffering from.

Is it mandatory to visualize? I would much prefer simplicity externally as well as mentally.

HH: It depends on the nature of the individual. So many questions arise: *What kind of meditation? Meditation on the nature of mind without thinking much? Simple concentration on the nature of mind? Then again, what level of nature?*

One aspect of the nature of the mind is colorless, formless, yet it is some kind of entity that has the quality of reflecting opposites. We cannot hold or imagine it, just like when a form is reflected in a clear mirror. But when the form is taken away, the reflection vanishes, too.

This is the same with the mind. It reflects the object. This is one level, one nature of the mind. For such meditation, there is no need for devotion and so on. Just concentrate on it daily and it will improve.

But here our goal is bodhicitta, altruism, a special kind of altruism: the understanding of emptiness, shunyata. It also prepares you for deity-yoga. Once one has received an initiation—the actual practice of Tantrayana is deity-yoga—one visualizes oneself as deities, and this builds a foundation for deity-yoga.

You say we are moving toward bodhicitta, toward higher truths, and using the deities to get us there, as an instrument. When moving to higher levels, does one always require intermediary symbols?

HH: Some people can have spontaneous realizations. This is possible for very exceptional practitioners. To such persons, it is said, realization and liberation come simultaneously.

Let us take the example of the meditation of bodhicitta. It seems that progress depends on one's merit. For example, two or three people practice the same teachings, try to achieve the same goal, and have the same level of knowledge. Although the facilities are the same, there are differences in the results. Within a short time, there could be a change of mental attitude in one of them, and the others change very slowly, although their circumstances are the same.

Knowledge and experience are different things, aren't they? Knowledge can be achieved through explanation, through reading and thinking. But we believe that for proper experience, you have to have merit, virtue. To a person with a great stock of merit or virtue either from past lives or from this life, things come easily. This is one reason for offering prostrations and so forth. Virtue arises and merits increase through these offerings. This is preparation. When you reach the actual practice of meditation, it becomes easier. This is one way.

As you mentioned, it is true that deity-yoga is known as simulated or artificial yoga. One finally reaches spontaneous yoga through the practice of simulated yoga.

But is it necessary?

HH: In order to reach spontaneous and nonstimulated yoga, one has to go through the process and stages of simulated and artificial yoga. That is why the Buddha has explained in tantra that simulated or artificial yoga is the boat by which to cross the river. The purpose of getting into the boat is not just to travel but to use it as a means to cross over to the other shore. Once you reach the shore of spontaneous yoga, you can leave the artificial behind. In this connection, one of the Tibetan masters said that although you have to abandon the boat sooner or later, the time of abandoning it is when you have reached the other side, and not when you are still on this side; but that depends entirely on the individual's experience.

According to some Tibetan traditions, this is possible just through direct investigation. But it is not investigation, is it? It is some kind of direct experience of purity of consciousness. According to that tradition, you use conceptual thought when you start to investigate. The proper way is without the disturbance of the mind, through basic consciousness, some kind of simultaneity, exceptional experience. That is very difficult. We say it is very easy, very powerful, this direct approach. But the actual experience is very difficult, although my experience is still very limited.

When one has such an experience, in those strong or very clear moments, one remembers events of past lives—not of one life but of hundreds of lifetimes. When these memories come up, a kind of highly subtle consciousness-experience becomes evident.

Sometimes such states of mind occur after great devotion, after many years of offering—for example, 100,000 prostrations, 100,000 mandalas, 100,000 recitations of the Hundred-Syllable Mantra. This is very hard work, a rigorous practice, and then spontaneous experiences occur on some special occasions. Although direct experience is the real aim, unless one prepares very rigorously for it, nothing will happen.

Why is it necessary to visualize the dissolution of deities into shunyata?

HH: It is necessary because one should be able to have a vision of the deity, the very consciousness that realizes emptiness appearing as a deity. It helps one in the training to see everything as a manifestation of emptiness. This refers to the emptiness of inherent existence. That very appearance of emptiness, that consciousness, which has the vision of emptiness, should be seen as the deity.

At the level of visual consciousness, they appear as a deity, their ordinary, mundane form. Does that not interfere with the consciousness of emptiness, which is what we are ultimately invoking?

HH: Although on the level of our sensorial consciousness, we have this ordinary appearance, what we are talking about here is to have the appearance of them in their pure nature, in their deity form on the level of mental consciousness, because the factors that have to be abandoned by training in the generation stage are ordinary appearances and ordinary perceptions. This ordinary appearance, however, is not the one that we have at the level of sensorial consciousness, which cannot be prevented anyway. We are talking of the appearance of the ordinariness of phenomena at the level of mental consciousness.

Just as we discussed in the meditation of samatha earlier, here we are not cultivating single-pointedness on the level of our sensorial consciousness, but on the level of our mental consciousness. It is done through mental consciousness. No matter what we see with our own eyes, if we make an effort to have an image of something else, we can visualize that image in our consciousness.

CHAPTER 14

THE ART OF TIBETAN MIND TRAINING

Your Holiness, the Tibetan tradition has very sophisticated mind-training techniques. Do you think that the mind can be trained in the same way as the body?

HH: From personal experience, I can tell you with confidence that the mind can be changed through training. When I was young, I was quite short-tempered; although it never lasted long, I used to lose my temper very often. Now, with training, and perhaps age, I have changed. Temper as well as attachment come and go, but without much effect on my basic monk mind. The mind is like an ocean: on the surface, waves come and go, but underneath, the ocean always remains calm.

The elimination of negative emotions is rather difficult; it needs a lot of effort, a lot of meditation and action. But it is possible to reduce the intensity of emotions. The ancient scriptures, their methods and techniques, are very relevant in today's world, irrespective of whether a person is a believer or a nonbeliever.

Many believe that money will solve all human problems. I believe that the answer to these problems is not external. Whereas the Western materialistic way of life or development is, of course, important and useful for humanity, traditional or spiritual values are equally, or more, important.

We should not neglect our own traditional richness. This inner richness is a combination of material development, physical comfort, as well as mental comfort through spiritual training. This should not be limited to Indians or Tibetans but should extend to humanity as a whole. For proper balance, material development and spiritual development must exist together.

In your opinion, why should one be convinced to train or change the mind? What would be its benefits?

HH: We should have a clear awareness of the benefits as well as the negative, harmful effects of the mind. We should have a clear recognition of the usefulness of compassion, love, contentment, and forgiveness; and that on the other side there is hatred, discontentment, attachment, which lead to problems.

Even from the point of view of physical health, the more compassionate the mind, the healthier we become. Compassion brings us inner strength and self-confidence, and these bring calmness. On the other hand, anger and hatred are very, very harmful for developing calmness or self-confidence.

When your mental attitude toward others is negative, they automatically have the same kind of attitude toward you. This leads to more fear, more doubt. So the result is uneasiness and unrest—a mental state very harmful for health.

The mind is like a successful life, or a happy family, in which different kinds of emotions are involved. The more compassionate, the more open-minded, bring more happiness to the home or community. However, anger and attachment are very important emotions. They are a part of daily life, and without them life becomes colorless. With these extra emotions, your life becomes more colorful.

Do you sometimes experience these kinds of emotions?

HH: Oh yes! Sometimes, of course! But actually, when you are mindful of these emotions, your mind becomes steady. As a result, your physical self also becomes very stable. Too many ups and downs are very harmful to the body.

So the demarcation between what is positive and what is negative is quite simple. Everybody has a desire to be happy and to live a fruitful life, and we should seek happiness as the very purpose of life. The positive emotions ultimately lead to happiness, calmness, and peace; while the negative ones bring suffering, either to others or oneself.

Your Holiness, Western traditions essentially use two strategies to help overcome mental distress: medication to change the biochemistry of the brain, or therapy where the patient talks to a therapist and articulates what may be hidden anxieties. What is the Tibetan tradition for training the mind?

HH: This essentially depends upon the case. Those people with serious physical imbalances should be cured by physical means. If it is purely psychological, one way to cure it, then, is to express what one is feeling. I usually feel there are instances when certain experiences in the past make one feel uncomfortable or fear something. In such cases, it may be helpful to express the anxieties.

When you see hatred or anger, basic negative emotions arise and continue to grow. It is very clear from my own experience that once you realize their negativity or harmfulness, you can take some kind of position or distance from them. That kind of attitude itself makes an impact on negative emotions. So, in some cases, it is better to control your emotions yourself.

Your Holiness, mental illnesses like depression and such are on the increase. Science addresses the biochemistry of the brain and uses drugs to cure them; you recommend the pursuit and practice of compassion as a "drug" for change. How do you reconcile the practice of meditation and the use of chemicals to alter states of the mind?

HH: It may be a little extreme to rely completely on meditation techniques to train the mind, but I feel that it is just as extreme to completely rely on external methods. Humans have a wonderful intelligence that should be utilized to alleviate illnesses, especially mental problems.

The human brain is like nuclear power, which can be used positively or destructively. Ultimately, this intelligence, this intellectual power, is of immense benefit if we use it properly. Meditation can also be of immense benefit to people suffering from mental illness.

The better way is to face the problem, tackle it from various aspects, and thereby reduce the mental burden. The problem may remain, but the mind achieves a measure of peace and calm, and the problem can be dealt with more effectively and positively.

Your Holiness, what exactly is tantra, especially in the context of Buddhism? Was it there from the time of the Buddha, or did it come later?

HH: It seems later. There is a system of belief according to which even Mahayana is not a direct teaching by the Buddha, and there is a general belief that tantra also came much later. On the other hand, if one does not accept Mahayana as an authentic teaching by the Buddha, then even Buddhahood itself is questionable. Therefore, one would more or less have to conclude that Mahayana is an authentic teaching by the Buddha. The difference is that the Buddha taught Mahayana to select audiences, not as public events. For some time, it remained a secret doctrine.

Tantra is even more secret. It also depends on the maturation of the karma of the practitioners; it is not necessary to restrict its emergence to the historical time of the Buddha Shakyamuni. According to the Mahayana view, although Buddha Shakyamuni passed away, he is still regarded as a living being. There are many stories of people who get direct teachings from the Buddha. Historically, some could see Buddha and receive teachings like that. In some cases

Buddha Shakyamuni appeared as a monk, in some cases as Vajradhara, a deity with the mandala.

Your Holiness, you have talked about mantras and the effect that they can have. Some of them help deepen your thinking and others your concentration. But I wonder how a series of sounds can actually do that . . .

HH: The oral repetition of the mantra, by sound, is the literal mantra. While we repeat the mantra, we are reflecting on the meaning of the mantra, which is deeper. How that type of recitation brings about those effects is difficult to explain. I think when we recite mantras properly, the merit increases. I don't know of any relation with sound.

Is it true that the vibrations of certain syllables also change the energy around and within us?

HH: Yes, it is possible. Another thing, of course, is the blessing. The mantra was taught by certain forces, and through the passage of time many people have practiced the same mantra. I think the mantra itself is blessed. Holy places are blessed by people or charged with some energy, and later the places will bless those who come there. The same is possible with mantras.

If one is engaged in the practice of wind yoga and visualizing channels and the like, there is a close link between them, which one can explain. Therefore, the main effect of the recitation of mantras comes in the practice of the highest Yogatantra in which one does the wind-and-channel yoga. That is one way of looking at it. Apart from that, I have no idea.

Your Holiness, the meaning of the word <u>mantra</u> is protection of the mind . . . that, in essence, it is positive, creative. One hears stories about people with evil intentions who use mantras to harm others. First of all, is that a possibility; and second, if it is a possibility, isn't it a contradiction?

HH: The possibility exists. Yantra, mantra—here when we talk of different activities such as peace, increase, influence, wrath, and so forth, they are different. There are a variety of practitioners; some are without any deep power of concentration, without altruism or understanding of shunyata. They can inflict harm through some kind of technique, but such power is rather limited.

Mantras are used for many different practices. There are also different kinds of mantras: for instance, those expounded by Vajradhara, the Buddha, in tantric treatises. There are other types that are expounded by worldly deities. It is very difficult to distinguish between non-Buddhist and Buddhist mantras. A distinction has to be made from the point of view of whether or not the complementary factors of wisdom exist, which understand shunyata and the altruistic attitude, the aspiration to help others achieve enlightenment. It is difficult to make that distinction from the mantra itself.

Different forms of deities, mandalas, and mantras, based on the theory of atman, are non-Buddhist. Those deities, mandalas, and mantras essentially based on anatman, shunyata, are Buddhist tantra.

CHAPTER 15

THE SCIENCE
OF THE MIND

There is no one Western view of mind, suffering, and healing. However, there is a commonality in Western views dating back to the radical period when Freud and Jung saw "mind" as submerged, with much less that was conscious and a lot that was unconscious. Today, the dominant view is based on the neuroscience model of the mind, which reduces "mind" to the physical processes of the brain.

Many Western pioneers criticize the Eastern approach to the mind as metaphysical rather than scientific or empirical. Even Jung, who was most sympathetic to Buddhist-Indian thought, said, "My conceptions are empirical and not speculative." What do you think?

HH: I think most of the Western views, and Jung and Freud, were wrong in one sense—they held that the mind in Indian-Buddhist thought is a metaphysical one. This is not true. The essence of the modern idea of the mind is internalization—that there is something within that causes suffering, which can also remove suffering. Suffering, therefore, does not come from outside. There are no spirits, ghosts, stars, and such. The Hindu system has the five passions, and the Buddhists have the *avidyas*, grasping attachments. So it is all inside, and that is very much the modern psychological idea of the mind. I think they were mistaken in confusing the historical for disproof.

The concepts of Indian philosophy are thoroughly philosophical. Western psychology tells you the story of modern European man's adventures. Only if you are able to see the relativity—that is, the uncertainty of all human postulates—can you experience that state in which modern psychology makes sense. But psychology just makes no sense unless you can empathize with beings who are forced to base their lives upon facts to be experienced and not transcendental postulates beyond human experience.

Your Holiness, will you please clarify the Buddhist concept of the mind?

HH: The use of the term *mind* is itself very tricky. The connotations in which I present this term may or may not conform to the word itself.

Here are some basic explanations from Buddhist thought. Some schools of Tantrayana talk of different levels of mind and body. According to what one calls "mind" or "consciousness," there are different levels and varieties. The grosser level of the mind is a product of the body. As long as the brain functions, this mind is active. As soon as the brain ceases to function, this mind will not function. It is physical and related to the chemical reactions of the brain. The basic nature of the mind is the clarity of knowing. In the Buddhist perception, there is another mind with a substantial cause, which is not related to the physical.

At the more subtle level, the mind experiences at an unconscious level. There is a very subtle energy that can separate us from our bodies. But frankly speaking, this is difficult to prove or speak about, unless one has some experience with meditation. So there are two categories of mind—the "grosser mind," which is dependent on the physical body; and a more "subtle mind," which is independent of the physical body.

It has happened that someone is declared clinically dead, but the body remains fresh, without decaying, for days. For example, for 13 days after his death, my own tutor's body remained fresh. In the early '70s, another practitioner's body remained fresh for 17 days after his death.

Our explanation is that the body and the brain functions cease, but the body remains fresh because the subtle mind is still in the body. As soon as the subtle mind departs from the body, the subtle way of control on the body is no longer there. After that, you see, some liquid appears and you see decay within minutes.

That is the concept of mind. Although we repeatedly use the words *mind, self, awareness,* or *consciousness,* our normal tendency is to use them without knowing what consciousness is.

Your Holiness, what is the self that constitutes the mind and the body?

HH: According to Buddhist scripture, the self should exist from within the aggregates and not as something unrelated or from somewhere else. Not all Buddhist schools accept an independent, partless, permanent self. But all Buddhists accept the third of what are known as the Four Seals of Buddhism, which says that all phenomena are empty and selfless.

Although this is the case, among the Buddhist schools, there are some that posit the existence of self. They identify the self with the five aggregates. Other schools, having difficulty identifying the self with the ordinary consciousness that is always changing from virtuous to nonvirtuous, posit a completely different consciousness, which has the qualities of a neutral, ever-present mind, called mind-basis of all. These schools identify the self with all the five aggregates or any of the five aggregates.

The Buddhist sage Chandrakirti says that the aggregates are like the possessions of the self. They are not the self itself; if the aggregates themselves were the self, the belongings and the person they belong to become one. The five aggregates are classified into two categories—*body* and *mind.*

We have this innate feeling that this body is my own possession—"my body." So, also, we can posit this body as belonging to the self or the object of enjoyment by the self. Similarly, we have this innate feeling of "my mind." The mind, too, can be looked upon as belonging to the self. Therefore, the self should be something different from the body and the mind. Although this is the case, when analytically sought, it cannot be found apart from the body and the mind.

On the other hand, if this self did not exist, there would be no human beings; there would be no point at all in having our discussions. Irrespective of whether we can find it or not, when analytically sought, there should be a self. Although the self does exist, we cannot find it when we analytically search for it, and this indicates that it does not exist independently.

If the self is not substantial, does it then become a dream, an illusion? Or is it a reality that exists?

HH: The question might arise that just as the self is an imputation or label, the man in the dream is also an imputation or label; so is there no difference between the two?

The answer is that both of them do not exist from the side of the object. They are both the same in that respect, but there is a difference in the way they exist as imputations. No harm can be inflicted by valid cognition trying to refute someone as a person, and he cannot be refuted as a person by wisdom, which searches for his ultimate nature.

However, although that very consciousness perceives the dream-man as a person, other types of consciousnesses can refute him. Although they are the same in the respect of not existing as objects, the difference is that one view can be dispelled by another consciousness, but the reverse cannot be done. Therefore, one exists as a person conventionally, and the other does not.

Since we established that the self exists and is not nonexistent, we have dispelled the extreme of nihilism.

And since we have refuted the existence of independent nature, we have also dispelled the extreme of eternalism. Through this, we achieve the middle way.

If it were possible to realize the mere absence of the independent self, could we perceive it? The answer would be yes, it can be perceived. Although it is a phenomenon that cannot be approached positively or from the side of affirmation, one can posit it by means of excluding its opposite factors.

For example, this table being devoid of elephant is something we cannot perceive affirmatively. But by excluding the object of negation—in this case, elephant —we can realize this table is free of elephant. Since the independent self is something that can be refuted by logical reasoning, we can have the certainty that there is no such self. The type of object of negation such as an inherent self or an independent self is nonexistent; and, therefore, it can be expelled by logical reasoning.

One might have the feeling that if the absence of independent nature is existent in all phenomena as inherent nature, what use is it to us to understand it? When things appear to us, we should ask how they appear to us. When the self appears to us, what kind of appearance does it have? Equally, with our friends, our enemies, a neutral person . . . when they appear to us, how do they appear? At that moment, although in nature the qualities of these persons are there, the differences are there. However, when they appear to us, that kind of quality never appears; they appear as solid, stable.

Someone may have the delusion that he can change the world. How can we distinguish when the mind is misleading us and when it is not? The mind is the tool we use for reasoning. When the mind itself is deluded, what can we do?

HH: There are two types of correct views—the correct view that is beyond the worldly level, and the correct worldly view:

— **First**, the view that is beyond the worldly level refers to the realization of the nature of phenomena, which means emptiness—that is, the appearance of phenomena as if they have some kind of inherent existence is a mistaken perception. Due to the influence of this mistaken perception, we have the apprehension of grasping at their true existence, which is also false. To know that our own consciousness that sees them is mistaken, we must first realize that phenomena themselves lack true existence. Through the realization of their nature, one can see that the consciousness to which phenomena appear in such a way is also mistaken.

When we experience emotional afflictions such as attachment or hatred, the object of our desire or repulsion appears as if it were something solid; the goodness or beauty of that object appears like something independent that will never change. Once we realize that the object of our attention does not really exist as we see it, our afflicted emotions of hatred or desire will be reduced. This is the stage where we meditate on emptiness.

— **Second**, in the correct worldly sense, consciousness that knows something is to be done in a certain way or something is to be done in another way unpolluted by such strong emotions is not related to the experience of strong emotions such as hatred and so on. Such a consciousness has to be judged on its own basis.

One often uses these terms interchangeably—self, mind, awareness, consciousness—and not in a very precise way.

HH: According to one Buddhist school of thought, there is a certain part of the mind we call "self," but the other Buddhist schools of thought do not agree with it. The "self" is something different from the "mind." But of course without the "mind," the "self" cannot exist. With a combination of the "body" and the "mind," you see the "self," the "being."

Your Holiness, you mentioned that this "I" is like a master. Is there something in us that makes us think or act—the ego? What is this "I" without which the human being is not able to act or think?

HH: That is the very problem. We cannot deny the existence of an "I." We cannot find it, but it does exist. It exists as a result of imputation. The self or "I" is not self-sufficient, but many of the ancient non-Buddhist schools explain it as a different entity from the aggregates. They say the body changes.

As far as the "I" is concerned, it is permanent, a sort of oneness. Buddhists do not accept such an "I." Such an "I"—we call it atman, and the very word *atman* symbolizes something solid or independent. Obviously, when our mind changes, the "I" changes automatically. When we have some pain, we can say, "I am sick," or "I have a pain." This is not the "I," but we can express ourselves through it.

Is it the same "I" that directs you to think in a particular manner?

HH: That agent is the consciousness. Abhidharmasamuccaya, a text by Asanga, deals with six types of mental factors. For example, there are five types of mental factors known as omnipresent mental factors, which accompany each primary mind: *feeling, recognition, intention, application of the mind to a certain object (decisive attention),* and *contact.*

Then there is mindfulness, aspiration, single-pointedness, and wisdom. Single-pointedness is not the same as the one talked about in samatha meditation. Each mental thought has an aspect that fixes the mind on the object. The minds have a factor that analyzes the object—that is, the factor of wisdom. Meditation, or samadhi, is mental tranquility, and special insight is the practice of wisdom.

We try to develop these two factors of the mind, the concentrative factor and the wisdom factor. There is a seed there, the Buddha-seed. When there is no seed, nothing can be produced, but the basis is there. Wisdom, deep samadhi or concentration, is possible because the potential exists.

Many different kinds of consciousness are explained. In one of the Burmese Buddhist texts, some 200 mental factors are enumerated. Although "I" is only a label imputed to the combination of mind and body, we identify our self more with consciousness because of our innate mind consciousness.

According to other Buddhist types of consciousnesses, concepts such as "my consciousness" are contradictory. Even when we talk about the conventional self, the "I," there are many different types. For example, when we say, "When I was a child," we get the feeling as if this "I" were a generality—an "I" that pervades the entire time from childhood until now. When we say, "At that time, I was very naughty, but now I have improved," we are confining the self to a certain span of time, and that type of self has already passed.

In this way, we can posit many different types of self or "I." According to the highest Buddhist schools of thought, the "I" is a mere label given to the aggregates of the body.

Your Holiness, what is the nature of the mind or personal identity that is retained in nirvana?

HH: This is quite difficult to explain. When we have purified all negative thought, there is still one being that has actually purified his or her own basic mind. Because it is completely purified, we call that the Buddha, or the purified one. Still there is someone who is actually purified. But there is no solid thing or the "I," which can feel . . . a state of no thought; once we achieve omniscience, there is no conceptual thought.

Your Holiness, the Buddhist approach to spirituality is also "rational"; it uses logical reasoning and follows investigation and experimentation, especially in dealing with the "mind." Please comment.

HH: My dialogues with scientists made it quite clear to me that the scientific field—in particular, cosmology, neurobiology, subatomic physics, and psychology—seems quite involved in Buddhist thought or philosophy. It would be useful to explain how these four scientific fields are relevant to, or connected with, Buddhist teachings.

Even within his own precepts, especially when leading or teaching disciples with different mental dispositions, the Buddha adopted different tactics for teaching. From the literal point of view, some of the teachings did not conform to reality. The Buddha stated that his followers should not accept his word out of faith but through investigation and experimentation.

The Buddha's urging not to accept his word blindly without investigation and experimentation gives one the liberty to examine his word. In this context, the Buddha's concept of the four reliances is significant.

According to this concept, it is more important to examine the authority of the teachings than the teacher or person who teaches the subject. With respect to the teachings, it is more important to pay heed to the meaning than the words. With respect to the meaning, we should give more importance to the ultimate meaning rather than the conventional or interpretive meaning. And finally, with respect to the realization of that ultimate meaning, it is more important to rely on the deeper understanding of wisdom rather than the conventional understanding of the mind.

Therefore, in Buddhism—in particular, the Mahayana teachings—it is extremely important to find and understand reasons rather than just accept the Buddha's words. Genuine followers or disciples of Buddhism are those with sharp mental faculties, who will not accept the Buddha's teachings merely because the Buddha teaches them. Rather, they examine the deeper meaning using logical reasoning, thereby ascertaining the authenticity of the teachings. Only after ascertaining the authenticity of the teachings will they be accepted.

The foundation of Buddhism rests on the Four Noble Truths. It is based on the law of causality—that is, change happens when there are causes and conditions for it. The Four Noble Truths are true suffering, causes of suffering, cessation of suffering, and the ways or methods of overcoming this suffering. Scientific thinking plays an important role in Buddhism.

The scientific way of examination and the Buddhist approach broadly follow a similar pattern. The First Noble Truth is that of true suffering. When we explain suffering and the three realms involved, we find connections with the science of cosmology. According to a Buddhist text, the world is flat. But according to modern science, it is clear that the world is round. As we can see and measure, we have the liberty to reject the proposition that the world is flat, using reason and direct experience.

The Buddhist explanation of how the world was formed using the five elements also has links with the science of cosmology. First, there was empty space or air with a kind of subtle energy. Through this subtle energy heat developed, and through heat a kind of liquid emerged. Finally, from this liquid came solid matter. The belief that solid matter eventually gives way to space and the cosmological theory of a limitless sort of world are similar.

The Second Noble Truth, the causes of suffering, is explained through the theory of karma or action, particularly in the context of the human experience of happiness and suffering, pain and pleasure. This is very closely related to motivation. Psychology is involved here and in the Fourth Noble Truth—that is, how to overcome ignorance or negative emotions. Through positive emotions, you can remove or reduce suffering.

In the field of negative emotions, modern psychology is relevant. In the connection between the brain and the mind, neurobiology is relevant. There are many interpretations of the Third Noble Truth, the cessation of suffering, that are profound or subtle. The Third Noble Truth is connected with the idea of emptiness. Here modern physics, particularly the quantum theory, is in some ways related.

This is not just my personal interest. The whole Buddhist structure, if properly examined, automatically generates a scientific approach.

CHAPTER 16

POLITICS OF CONFLICT
AND RELIGION

Your Holiness, do you consider yourself to be more a politician or a religious leader?

HH: I have always considered myself a simple Buddhist monk. I think my very nature is closer to that of a spiritual practitioner. From birth, I have not believed I have the proper qualities of leadership. I don't think so! In modern politics, especially, I feel there is too much politeness, too much of it. Sometimes I'm really bored. I love to have fun and speak in a straightforward, friendly manner.

As a spiritual master who also wears a political robe, what is the ideal relationship for your two halves—the one that works best?

HH: Tibetan freedom is very closely related to Buddhist Dharma, so I personally consider my involvement with the freedom struggle as part of my spiritual practice, because it directly benefits a large number of people. From the Buddhist point of view, this would not only be for this life, but for life after life, beyond this one.

In fact, it is now quite clear that Tibetan freedom does not only mean political freedom, but also the freedom of spiritual practice, spiritual teaching, and studies. So I often say to my Buddhist friends in the West, "You have a very good knowledge of Buddhist Dharma and practice it very sincerely. Yet for the next generation or two, at least, without a Tibet you cannot hold the complete Buddhist Dharma, which we traditionally keep." Hopefully, after a few generations, it may be different. Therefore, the question of the existence of a complete form of Buddhist Dharma on this planet is dependent on Tibetan freedom.

I have always believed that we need an attitude of pluralism in religion. This is essential. So while I'm involved in the freedom struggle for national freedom, I always promote the idea of pluralism, a pluralistic attitude toward religion. For the last three to four centuries, there have been several thousand Muslims and 100,000 Christians living in Tibet, and I believe the spirit of harmony, based on mutual understanding and respect, is taking proper shape.

How do you reconcile with the amount of conflict and war in the name of religion?

HH: It is very sad. I think it creates a negative impression of all the religions of this world. However,

I do believe in this modern age, the age of technology, that the value of religious traditions is still there. I also see that the values of various religious traditions have remained intact. In fact, I believe that as more and more material progress takes place, the limitations of materialist values will also become clearer. Under such circumstances, the value of spirituality will also become clearer, more significant.

Therefore, we can all benefit from the useful messages and techniques of various religious traditions. Having said that, I must reiterate that killing one another in the name of religion is very sad.

Many today blame the politicization of religion for rampant violence and intolerance and question whether politics should mix with religion. What is your opinion?

HH: I believe there is a difference. Political institutions and religious institutions should be separate; it is safer if they are separate. Yet a combination of religious and temporal work can happen together.

From my own experience in dealing with official duties, I see where people can be hurt or helped, and I know that I must be careful and do what is correct by Dharma. A religious belief is very helpful to maintain honesty. Moreover, the experience I gain from practical areas benefits me religiously. I don't know how it will be in the future, but for now, the dual responsibility is very helpful.

Some time ago, I was at a seminar in India. Some politicians said, "We are politicians; we are not religious." Some said this with humility, some were showing off.

I said jokingly, "Politicians *should* be religious because what is in their minds will influence the people they serve. On the other hand, if religious people remain alone on mountains and their minds are corrupt, it is of little concern because they will not affect the public."

If the right thinking is followed, even warfare would be less destructive. It is like the five fingers of our hand, in which each finger may have its special capacity and function, but without the palm it is useless. Similarly, every human activity, such as religion, science, economy, and education, pursued with sincere motivation and human affection, can be positive. This includes politics.

What, after all, is politics? Politics is not necessarily cheating or bullying. Rather, I think there is a certain kind of precise meaning in politics. It is another human activity or another instrument to serve society, the community, or the nation.

You see, by itself there is nothing wrong in it, but it is dependent on the motivation or the behavior of those who are involved in politics. Even in religion, if the motivation is not genuine, religion becomes dirty. On the other hand, when the individual in politics acts with sincere motivation, it is spiritual practice. So from my perspective, every human action that is conducted with sincere, honest motivation can be considered a spiritual activity.

When Dharma becomes an individual's way of life, whatever that person might be involved in—politics or religion—it works for the benefit of others.

However, if practiced together, do you feel that the risk of communalism sharpens? What does it mean to be truly secular?

HH: Religion has to be explained on the basis of the type of motivation one has. From that point of view, we see the benefit of religion on many aspects of human society.

If politics is carried out by religious-minded people, maybe there would be healthier politics. If that is the context, there is no problem, and politics and religion should be combined. But in the case of religious institutions (not a religion, but an institution), someone who works both in religious institutions and politics may create a negative impact.

As a Buddhist monk, I believe that the ultimate important thing is motivation, sincere motivation. One should think of the common interest rather than the individual interest. The right way is to think for the benefit of the majority. That's the proper way of human thinking.

We are social animals. Our own future and prosperity depends on other human beings. Concepts such as modern economy and globalization show that everything is interdependent. Therefore, the very concept of "we" and "they" is no longer meaningful.

The entire humanity, the entire world, is a part of you. I think that is the reality.

There should be a sense of concern for others. It is the proper way of thinking about the nature of humanity and about the nature of the world. That's the prime motivation—and with that motivation, teach religion . . . pursue politics, scientific research, economics. Every human activity should be governed by that kind of motivation. Only then can every human action be positive.

Your Holiness, there is great concern in India about the endless violence in Kashmir and the future of Indo-Pakistani relations. Globally there is conflict in Bosnia, Lebanon, the Middle East, and so on. Where do you think the solutions lie to conflicts of this nature?

HH: Very difficult! I have no clear answer. Of course, I do feel concern for the suffering of individuals involved in conflicts in Bosnia, in east and west Africa, and in Kashmir; they are terrible. I feel sadness for the Kashmir problem within India, too.

I first came to India as a refugee in 1959, and when I reflect on the experiences at that time, there was a genuine peace, with the *ahimsa* tradition still very much alive. Now I sometimes jokingly tell my Indian friends, "Throughout the centuries, you produced and kept ahimsa as your philosophy. Now you export these values, and too much export has reduced it in your own country."

I am very concerned about what is happening here. We all need long-term plans and solutions. Sometimes the short-term methods may not seem to be acceptable but might need to be tolerated for the long-term benefits. I just find it very sad that we have now degenerated from the centuries-old ahimsa philosophy. This is very sad.

CHAPTER 17

UNIVERSAL
RESPONSIBILITY

Your philosophy of universal responsibility has made a central contribution to secular dialogue and has even been endorsed by the Nobel Committee. Will you clarify this philosophy for us?

HH: In ancient times, some religious teachings said that we must develop altruism or practice altruism as a matter of virtue or ethics. Today, I feel the circumstances are entirely different, because the world—due to technology and also the population—has become much smaller. Some events may happen on one side of the world and its repercussions or effects are felt on the other. We depend heavily on one another. Today altruism is a practical necessity.

In economic and environmental fields, also, countries depend heavily on one another. The concept of "we" and "they" is out-of-date. We should consider the whole world as "we" or "us." However, the reality is that because of a lack of awareness and analytical meditation, this has not happened. We still believe in separateness. I feel that many problems happen because of this kind of narrow-mindedness and shortsightedness.

For instance, we now face a serious, worldwide ecological problem; and no matter how powerful one or two nations are, the issue will not be resolved without joint effort or a common position. In a modern economy, there are no national boundaries; and in certain fields, like health or education, there is already unification.

My own interest, my own future, and my own nation's future are very much related with other people. But human thought is still very concerned about "my" nation, "my" nationality, "my" national boundary. Reality has changed, but our concept has not caught up. It is not even getting close to reality, and this is one cause for problems.

Obviously, for the six billion members of humanity, this small planet is our only hope, and we all have the responsibility to look after it as a whole. I believe we need a sense of "global" and "universal responsibility." When that is established, our attitude toward other minor problems—economic, religious, or cultural—will be more easily tackled. I advocate the practice and implementation of that kind of spirit.

The remedy is that we must catch up with that reality. Human attitude must develop, must change, and must embrace reality. We need a sense of global responsibility, a sense of universal responsibility. With that we can solve many man-made problems or at least minimize them.

I think the logic is quite simple! You see, my interest very much depends on others' interests. Unless I take

care of others' interests, I will not benefit. If I ignore others' interests, ultimately I will lose and suffer. If we take
more care about others' rights, others' interests, ultimately we all benefit.

Why is that?

HH: Quite simple! Today there are about 6.7 billion
people on the planet. In reality, a majority of them are
not genuine believers. Of course, people say, "I belong,
or my family belongs, to this tradition or that tradition,"
but in their daily lives they are not necessarily believers.
So, the majority are nonbelievers, and at the same time
the majority is a very important part of humanity.

When a child is born into a religion, it is born without faith. Even when the parents perform rituals, the
child has no feeling for, or appreciation of, those actions.
The child's mind is free from any faith and survives with
human affection and concern. The mother's physical
touch or the giving of milk is what the child appreciates.
These are very strong feelings of appreciation, of human
affection. Without these, the child cannot survive. So,
therefore, from birth I think humanity is not free from
human affection.

So is that the basis of your secular spirituality?

HH: That's right. I believe that basic human nature
is gentleness, gentleness based on that kind of human
affection. If our minds remain calm, compassionate, and
open-minded, the physical condition remains healthy. If

there is constant frustration, anger, agitation, and hatred, these things affect the mind and eventually drain our health.

This shows in the very nature of the body. It is compatible with the peaceful mind, the compassionate mind, but not the agitated mind. It is much better to carry out our work with a gentle, affectionate nature; and I believe that nature is the essence of every human being. We experience that nature from birth, but I believe that as we grow up, we place more emphasis on the brain and the intellectual side of our nature and neglect our basic human quality. Consequently, the brain overwhelms our good nature, and I believe that is the reason we are experiencing so many problems in the world.

In the 20th century alone, we have adopted various methods that have relied predominantly on machines, and their limitations are showing up. The time has come when we have to return to our basic human qualities, our basic human nature. We continue to promote the intellectual or knowledge side of our nature, but the virtuous human qualities must also increase. We must make an effort to see that the human brain and the human heart are performing in balance. That's my meaning of secular ethics.

The concept of sentient beings is central to Buddhism. You have taken it into the international arena and suggested that we should have rights for all sentient beings. Can you clarify?

HH: I feel that taking care of the environment of this planet is something like taking care of our own future.

This planet is our home, yet scientists have a vision to explore other planets such as Mars and build dwellings there. Of course, it may be possible; but ultimately this blue planet is our only home. We must take steps to protect it and every living creature and thing that makes up this planet.

It is wrong to exploit any part of the environment, disregarding its natural beauty and balance in order to make money. It is a foolish, shortsighted vision that leads to long-term destruction. We should recognize the unifying "life" within all sentient beings and develop the attitude that shows the same respect to all aspects of the environment that we would show our own families.

If we disregard the needs and feelings of these living, sentient beings, our minds will also be negatively influenced about our fellow human beings. We will see them as weak, worthless, and not deserving of respect. All life is sacred! There will be a gradual influence or gradual change through various influences. Therefore, I feel that compassion or respect toward all forms of life is the basis of a genuine sense of compassion or sense of caring toward humanity.

Would you, then, suggest a reworking of the Universal Declaration of Human Rights to include rights of the environment and rights of all sentient beings?

HH: I think the time has come when we should make an effort to develop that kind of attitude. I think that step is very necessary. The environmental issue is important. The inhabitants of this planet can now see the consequences of carelessness and abuse to the environment.

Scientists are seeing the effects of pollution on mothers' milk and, consequently, on the new generation. Scientists are also recognizing that the effects of our abuse of the planet and the environment are not limited to human beings.

We must develop the virtue of compassion for everything—humanity as a whole, the environment, each other, and ourselves. It is a great shame that people look at the practice of compassion as something not relevant in our day-to-day lives.

*The following set of conversations were recorded
in March and April 2008, during and soon after the
protests and demonstrations in Tibet—the largest since
1959—and in several cities around the world, as the
Olympic torch traveled across five continents during
the countdown to the Beijing games. The issue of
Tibet took center stage in the global media
and in the conscience of the free world.*

*The conversations took place prior to the death
of the Dalai Lama's brother, Taktser Rinpoche,
in September 2008.*

CHAPTER 18

THE TIBET QUESTION

Do you feel anger or upset at the unfolding situation in Tibet?

HH: Sometimes an angry thought does enter my mind. But essentially I do not experience anger; it is alien to me. Anger means wanting to harm someone—I am able to dismiss the thought easily and quickly. My practice helps me overcome negative emotions and find equanimity—it involves a process of giving and taking. I receive Chinese mistrust, and I send out compassion. I must admit that it hasn't always been easy for me in recent weeks.

What do you do to cope with this trying time?

HH: Despite all the fears and worries, I am at peace with my subconscious, so I can perform my duties quite normally. I have no trouble sleeping. Perhaps this is because I also pray for the Chinese, for their leadership, and for those who carry out bloodshed. I pray that their veils of ignorance might lift and they can be freed from their negative karma and the consequences of their actions.

Does the Dalai Lama ever weep?

HH: I was with Professor Samdhong Rinpoche, our prime minister of the exiled government, when I heard news of the terrible violence in Tibet inflicted by the Chinese. We had tears in our eyes.

How do you feel when the Chinese describe you in very harsh language, even calling you a criminal?

HH: If doing this makes them happy, they can carry on. What I condemn most is when the Chinese authorities force the Tibetans in Tibet to abuse me with threats and compel them to denounce me in writing.

What is the most disturbing aspect of the Chinese "campaign"?

HH: Chinese propaganda and manipulation of the media and news. They are creating a picture of racial discrimination in which all Tibetans are against all the

Chinese. This is not true. Before the 1950s there were Chinese in Lhasa and there was no problem—even after 1959 there was no anti-Chinese feeling. After that, some signs of resentment toward Han Chinese began in Tibet. This is unfortunate.

Whenever Chinese come to see me, I welcome them, and most of them cry. They are devoted and friendly.

In the 1990s, the main reason for my visit to Taiwan was to show that we are not anti-Chinese; we respect them, respect their rich cultural heritage, and admire their civilization. Above all, it is very important to develop a spirit of friendship with the Chinese people as our neighbors. Now I am sad that this Chinese propaganda will further create problems.

As a young man, what was your first response to the provocations and hostility of the Chinese? Has it been easy for you to arrive at this compassionate attitude toward those whom most people would see with hatred and with anger as their enemy?

HH: In 1950, the Chinese army entered Tibet, the part that was controlled by the Tibetan government. Earlier, although the Chinese army had already reached the eastern capital of Tibet, there was no Chinese influence and no Chinese office in Lhasa. According to historical record, Tibet was an independent nation when the Chinese army marched in.

More than 8,000 Tibetans had already been killed. I was anxious that the Chinese People's Liberation Army should be stopped, and the Chinese government also realized it might be better for them if Tibet could be "peacefully liberated." In 1954, I went to China as a member of the Tibetan delegation to a caucus of the Chinese people and the Chinese Communist Party. During that period, I had several meetings with Chairman Mao, who was a wonderful revolutionary. At that time, I developed a genuine respect for him. I admired him, and I also received useful advice from him.

What advice did you receive from him?

HH: He mentioned that the Communist Party is like a fish, and a fish cannot survive without water. Similarly the Communist Party cannot survive without criticism.

On another occasion, he asked me whether there was a Tibetan flag or not. I was a little hesitant and answered yes. He told me that the Tibetan flag must always be flown beside the Chinese national flag. Chairman Mao said that in ancient times Tibet was a great nation, but then we had become very weak. According to him, we could develop within 20 years, and then it would be our turn to help them.

He also told me that he would send two generals to stay in Tibet, in order to help me. In case these generals did not listen properly to my wishes, I was to let him know and he would withdraw.

I even mentioned to some Chinese officials that I wanted to join the Chinese Communist Party. There were some Tibetans who had joined the party. Later, one of my old Communist friends told me that at that time the Chinese leadership had genuinely felt that with the help of the Chinese, we Tibetans could ourselves build a modern Tibet.

When I was returning to Lhasa in 1955, I met a general coming from Tibet on the same road. I knew this general and told him how the previous year when I was coming to Peking [Beijing] by road, I was suspicious and fearful, and how I was happy and surprised that now, after almost one year, I was coming back to my country with full confidence in the Chinese. But soon after, as a result of continuing Chinese oppression, many Tibetan Communists, especially those from remote areas in Tibet, expressed their resentment and unhappiness over Chinese actions. They were dismissed from their posts, and many were put in prison and tortured. I was very disillusioned.

In 1956, I came to India to attend a conference. Although I had on several occasions met with Pandit Nehru, on one occasion the Chinese premier also joined us. He told us that he did not consider Tibet as just another Chinese province, but that its case was a special one.

Given your fears, what prompted you to return?

HH: The unrealistic reforms that took place in China resulted in an uprising in Tibet, also. Chairman Mao had promised a six-year postponement of the reforms in Tibet. At that time, I discussed with Pandit Nehru whether I should stay in India or not. Nehruji came up with the seven-point agreement and advised me that I should return to Tibet and fight. I listened to this advice and returned in February 1957. I tried my best to carry out this work according to the advice of Pandit Nehru and some other freedom fighters.

But the situation worsened. I tried my best to cool it down, but both sides were equally determined. In March

1959, the Tibetan people began to pour into Lhasa from the villages, and many feared that my life was in danger. The situation escalated from March 10, as the Chinese side remained determined to crush the Tibetan people.

I pleaded with the Tibetans to go back to their villages and said that if they wanted, some representatives could remain. Their numbers were aggravating the situation and making the Chinese more nervous and suspicious. The Tibetan side was determined to stay and defend its capital city. I was suspended in between. Fearing a bloodbath in Lhasa, and thinking that I could more usefully serve the Tibetan cause by leaving for some time so that the situation could be defused, I finally escaped to India and became a refugee.

Give us a brief background on your recent political negotiations with China.

HH: In the late '70s and early '80s, the Chinese sent messages to my elder brother in Hong Kong asking to meet in Peking.

I saw it as a positive indication and conveyed to him our decision of seeking autonomy for the entire Tibetan population. A two-hour-long meeting was held with Tang Jiaxuan, who was open to the discussion of every subject except independence. The meeting was a success, and as a result, four to five fact-finding delegations visited Tibet in 1979–80. Hoya Ma visited Hazra in 1980 and publicly acknowledged destruction, and apologized for the mistakes committed in the past by the Chinese. Conditions at that time had taken on a truly positive tone, and things looked very hopeful.

The top five Chinese officials at that time sent a five-point proposal, according to which an official was to visit me in Delhi, all privileges prior to 1959 were to be restored, the Dalai Lama was to remain in Peking and could occasionally visit Tibet. I rejected this outright, stating that the main issue here was the basic rights of the six million Tibetan people, and unless that was addressed, talking about my return was irrelevant.

What prompted you to agree to send your first delegations to Tibet in the 1980s?

HH: In 1983, I once again expressed publicly my desire to visit Tibet and decided to send a delegation in 1984 to make the required preparations, as I did not wish my visit to cause unrest. I recall when the first delegation reached Lhasa, the whole population of the area came to greet them. Even those who had posed as great revolutionaries during the Cultural Revolution were among the first to welcome the delegation.

So in 1984 we sought Chinese permission to send a delegation to Tibet to make preparations for my visit. But the Chinese found it difficult to accept it. Formal contact with the Chinese continued until 1993, with a few occasional meetings taking place in Delhi. Then in 1993 all contact ceased.

What happened then?

HH: We were not in direct touch with them until 2002. And since then, we have had six rounds of talks.

At the third, they presented to us a list of 36 accusations. At the fourth, we cleared them all point by point, since most of them were baseless. But the whole exercise proved to be very fruitful for us. It gave us a better understanding of how the Chinese saw us and what their fears were—basically that we were indirectly seeking independence from China.

Were you able to reassure them that this was not true?

HH: At the fifth round, in February 2006, the Chinese delegation acknowledged that we were not seeking independence. We saw it as marked progress in our confidence-building effort, and they also stated that regarding past history, the differences in opinions between the two sides were many. However, in April/May 2006 they intensified their propaganda on how we were encouraging separatists in Tibet. This was a deliberate campaign.

I believe the Chinese party secretary in the autonomous region of Tibet said that what isolates Tibet from China is Tibetan Buddhism, Tibetan culture. So, personally speaking, if those who have real power have this kind of view, then they obviously cannot be expected to protect and preserve Tibetan Buddhism, culture, and its environment.

What help are you expecting from other nations?

HH: I made a special appeal on behalf of six million Tibetans inside Tibet, especially those in rural areas who are completely isolated. I want to inform the world community that the Tibetan nation is a unicultural heritage facing extinction. Tibet is an ancient nation; please help us in preserving it.

I describe this as a kind of cultural genocide, whether intentional or unintentional. For instance, they have intentionally placed restrictions on Tibetan studies and on Tibetan monasteries. Tibetan culture is based on Buddhism, so these institutions are very, very important for the preservation of Tibetan culture. With the kind of restrictions on these, it is actually a form of genocide.

By increasing the Chinese population, for example, in Lhasa, where it has now crossed 200,000, Tibetans are becoming a minority. So if two-thirds of the population is Chinese in the towns of Tibet, everyone will have to speak Chinese to work or shop. The Chinese population in Tibet is increasing month by month, so demographic aggression is very serious.

I notice that Tibetans born elsewhere are able to preserve the Tibetan cultural heritage much better than those in Tibet. Those from Tibet are now becoming short-tempered; although they have a strong Tibet spirit, some show clear signs of degeneration. Ours is a peaceful, compassionate cultural heritage; and it is now degenerating. So this is very, very serious.

I hear of large-scale deforestation, as a result of which unprecedented floods happened in China. Maybe some government officials have a respect for the environment, but private businessmen do not care for the government's instructions and continue deforestation and mining. We therefore must have autonomous authority to preserve the Tibetan cultural heritage, Buddhist faith, and the environment.

Our friends—including the Europeans, Americans, and Japanese—can help to reach the solution, but the mutual agreement must be between Chinese and Tibetans.

Were you opposed to the Olympics being hosted in China?

HH: When the decision on the venue for the next Olympics was made, I openly expressed that as the most populated and ancient nation, China deserves to host the games. It will make them proud as a people, and so the games must be held there. Since we are not anti-Chinese, we respect the decision of China being the venue for the Olympic Games.

However, we must also acknowledge some of the criticisms that many individuals, nongovernmental organizations (NGOs), and governments have made about the Chinese record on human rights and religious freedom. The record is very poor. In the meantime it is very important to remind Chinese leaders and concerned officials that in order to be the respected hosts of the game, they must seriously improve their records in the field of human rights, religious freedom, and the environment.

How did you respond to the unprecedented protest and opposition in Tibet that happened, for example, in March 2008?

HH: Of course I understood the impatience of the young. I have been familiar with such dreams for many years, and I had hoped that they had subsided long ago. The youth have no concept, just emotions.

Aside from the moral question of violence, what would this mean for them if Tibetans take up arms to achieve their independence? Which arms, and where would they come from? And if we get the weapons, how do we get them to Tibet? And once that armed war of independence has begun, who will come to our aid?

I understand the protests—without supporting them, of course. I also counseled the organizers of the so-called peace march from here in Dharamsala to the border of the People's Republic, asking them to cancel their plan, because it could lead to clashes with the armed border guards. But all I can do is give advice, not suppress opinions. I can only hope that the Chinese will not use this as an excuse to commit another bloodbath.

So what in your view led to that situation within Tibet?

HH: Clearly the Chinese must finally admit that there is a Tibet problem. This overwhelming rejection of the Communist Party government and its policies can't be ignored anymore. Beijing needs to accept that something has gone terribly wrong in the last 50 years.

Unlike earlier unrests, this time they affected Lhasa, the so-called Tibet Autonomous Region (TAR), and all over. The protests spread to all Tibetan-speaking parts of China, including Tibetan students at Beijing universities. Also, after years of oppression, the Tibetans no longer trust the Chinese.

The Chinese have tried everything—oppression and torture, political reeducation, political indoctrination, and increasing the Han Chinese population in Tibet—but all have failed. Even programs to improve the standard of living and pouring money into infrastructure projects only show that Tibetans value their cultural independence and spirituality far more.

Why did you give up the cause of Tibetan independence for autonomy?

HH: The Tibetan ethnic groups are spread all over the Chinese provinces instead of only the present area that is designated an autonomous region only in name, without any autonomy. So we decided to discuss with the Chinese not the issue of our independence, but within the Chinese nation a single autonomous region that would help preserve our culture and language, instead of many small autonomous regions.

So we decided in principle that we would not seek independence but keep the real spirit of the middle path as our goal. This idea became very acceptable as a reasonable proposition in the public domain, and many countries have supported this. It has been the focus of our talks from our side.

Many supporters feel that you have sold out by adopting your final middle-path position as a negotiating one. You have no concessions to make in striking a deal with the Chinese.

HH: I respect the Chinese nation. I believe in an honest, transparent dialogue and not playing games.

In the Chinese provinces of Hunan, Sikang, Gansu, and Sinkiang, the Tibetan population is around four million. The Tibetan population in the Tibetan Autonomous Region is around two million, so the majority of Tibetans are outside Tibet. Tibetan ethnic groups are spread all over the Chinese provinces, so instead of autonomous regions, why not have a single autonomy?

I have tried to reason with these groups by giving them two choices: one of an independent Tibet geographically defined by the present Tibetan Autonomous Region that will exclude many Tibetans; or of a Greater Tibet, including my own place of birth, that is united and autonomous, with complete guarantee of the preservation of our identity, culture, and language. Some sensible Tibetans chose not the first but the second option. A single entity is really worthwhile.

You see, my own birthplace is now under Chinese administration, so legally even I am Chinese. For the Chinese, I am a devil, and the Tibetans see me as selling Tibetan rights.

Since "autonomy" best reflects your spiritual commitment to the middle path, how would you argue its political merit to all?

HH: Autonomy for Tibet offers the best options. My approach is not separation, but to stay within the People's Republic of China with full protection for our unicultural heritage, including our language and delicate environment.

Also, to remain within China is in our own best interest. Spiritual advancement alone cannot fill our stomachs; we also need modern development. So while if Tibet remains within China, it is beneficial, it is only so if we have meaningful authority and a full guarantee to protect our special needs.

The Tibetans must have the power to decide on all issues relating to culture, religion, and the environment. This is different from being an independent state. Under international law, this new Tibet would also be part of the People's Republic of China, which would remain responsible for foreign and security policy. If Beijing would agree to such a model, I can guarantee that we would no longer have such unrest and such a crisis as we have now.

Is there any risk in this option?

HH: There is a risk that the Chinese leadership believes that it no longer stands a chance of pacifying Tibet, and that it has lost the loyalty of the Tibetans forever. At the same time, the Chinese want to completely control a country with such rich natural resources. In that case, they will oppress our people even more brutally, eventually turning them into an insignificant minority in their own homeland. The latter option is a Tibet for Han Chinese. It would be the end of all dialogue with us and the end of all measures to build trust.

Yet many Tibetans criticize your middle path and perhaps even oppose it . . .

HH: As Pandit Jawaharlal Nehru used to say to me often, the state is for the people and by the people. I have always held this view. In 1993, contact with the

Chinese ceased, and I asked the Tibetan community for their opinion. Since 2001, we have an elected parliament, so the final decision is in their hands. I am acting as a senior advisor.

But many people are critical of my middle path, including my elder brother, who says that his dear younger brother Dalai Lama has now sold out Tibetan rights. I respect him as my eldest brother, but his political view is different. So not only among Tibetans but also among my supporters some are very critical of our approach; they always talk of independence—it is understandable that they are concerned about Tibet. I am committed to the middle approach. So if the Dalai Lama approach fails, their frustration increases.

Unfortunately, Chinese leaders do not understand what freedom is, what democracy is. Some Tibetans also have no experience, and they choose different expressions. The Chinese then accuse us, asking why they are not controlled. I say we cannot control—we do not *want* to control—people. The democratic principle is now deeply ingrained in us.

I follow Buddha: Buddha never says do this, do that, but gives us liberty. He asks his followers not to respect his teachings out of devotion, but by experimenting themselves.

So our real master, Buddha, also says this.

Is it then not possible that in the future other voices will try to challenge your middle approach and seek full independence?

HH: As far as our approach is concerned, the whole world knows that the Dalai Lama is not seeking independence. Only the Chinese don't know this.

Now if this approach fails, then we will ask our people what to do, since some of our supporters prefer independence. This is the democratic way. We are fully committed to democracy, and some of these youth are rather tough. I cannot ask them to keep quiet, nor can I say we must do as I want. It is their right to express what they feel, but it is my responsibility to make clear the consequences of any action they choose. My moral responsibility is clear to them. So, it is their human right and freedom to criticize my approach, my elder brother included.

There is serious frustration inside Tibet. In recent years Tibetans from Tibet—even those with a good livelihood, like students educated in China—express a lot of frustration. I believe Tibetans between the ages of 30 and 40, the younger generation, say that so long as the Dalai Lama is there, they have to follow my advice, but after he is gone, then they have to take appropriate action.

I feel bad about these kinds of expressions. So whenever I meet them, I always emphasize that they should concentrate on education and economics and training. I urge them to make appeals to local authorities to facilitate their education. We have a right to appeal for these things.

While the Chinese acted brutally in Tibet, the Tibetan youth have also sometimes participated in acts of looting and arson in Lhasa.

HH: I assume that this was the case. I condemn it, and it makes me sad to see my fellow Tibetans acting in this way—even though it was most certainly the result of deep-seated disillusionment and despair over being second-class citizens in their own country. But this is no excuse for violence.

I proposed an international investigation of the events in Tibet by a recognized, independent institution. But one thing is certain: it was, for the most part, innocent Tibetans who suffered under the brutality of the police and military. We deplore the loss of all life, whether Chinese or Tibetan. We lack a complete and detailed picture of what happened and is still happening in Tibet.

There are many distortions—we heard that 500 Chinese soldiers shaved their heads and dressed in monks' clothing to create trouble. I believe there may have been instances stemming from strong emotions, but Tibetans are genuinely peaceful and nonviolent.

Do you hope for a solution through talks with China?

HH: Indeed, talks for the sake of talks, about talks, are pointless. I am only interested in serious discussions to address the core of the problems. They are highly welcome, and without preconditions. But they must be conducted in a way that is transparent for the outside world—enough of the secret talks behind closed doors. Of course, the international pressure on Beijing has worked to some degree. The whole world must help us. The Chinese are very concerned about their international reputation.

It is not sufficient just to talk. I welcome neutral and respected people with free access to travel in the affected areas to do a thorough investigation, accompanied by the media.

Both China and India have become part of Tibet's political and spiritual reality. How do you compare them?

HH: People have to follow the modern way; democracy is not perfect, but it is the best for our times, and that is what India follows. Here, the south, north, west, and east have different languages, different sorts of food. Yet, except to some extent in a few pockets, the entire country stays happily together. How? Not by force. This is because of the rule of law, freedom of expression, and different sorts of freedoms. So in India there is stability because even if something small happens, it comes out in the newspaper. On the other hand, China looks stable, but underneath there is resentment; it is a police state.

In today's world, the rule of terror cannot achieve lasting peace, progress, or development. Harmony must come from the heart, not out of a gun. How can we develop harmony and unity through violence? Impossible. With more terror, there is more pain; it is the source of disunity. I think Chinese leaders should study human psychology.

Did you feel let down by the Indian government's response to that crisis?

HH: We take a holistic view of the position of the Indian government and people, with whom we have emotional and mental ties despite the physical control of the Tibetans by the Chinese.

Fifty years ago Pandit Nehru had initiated policies for Tibetan refugees, and every government, whether Bharatiya Janata Party or the Congress Party, has followed the same policies. There are programs for modern education, various activities for preserving and promotion of Buddhist culture and studies. It's due to them that we have our own community—and that, too, a healthy one. We have been able to preserve our culture, religion, and traditions. So as long the Buddhist religion is preserved and Tibetans remain in majority, that's the biggest help India can give.

Our young boys and girls, who are able to shout today—it is largely due to India's commitment to freedom of expression. The other day I spoke to the leaders of the Tibetan protestors in India who were protesting against the Chinese. I told them I am personally committed to democracy and believe in freedom of speech, movement, and thought.

I have no right to stop them or ask them to shut up, but I do have the moral responsibility to make them aware of the consequences of their actions. We must not do anything that will seriously compromise the government and people of India, who have been so generous to us.

Hearing of the militant protests in Tibet, you were quoted as saying that "if things go completely out of hand, I will resign." Can you hand over the temporal/spiritual roles of the Dalai Lama just like that?

HH: I am already in a semiretired position, so it is possible that soon I may resign fully. In our political field, every five years we hold elections. On the spiritual side, a young, healthy, qualified leadership will come, so I have no worry. These young, qualified spiritual leaders will take care of Buddhism and Buddhist culture. Therefore, as one old monk, I should now devote more time for the preparation of my next life. Isn't it so?

For Tibetans in general and Tibet in particular, your role is both central and critical, as is the office of the Dalai Lama. What about the future? If you resign, will the next Dalai Lama be a reincarnation, or will you choose your own successor?

HH: As early as 1969, I had stated that the Dalai Lama's institution, whether it should continue or not, should be decided by the Tibetan people. Earlier there have been instances where the present leader before his death has chosen his successor who is a good, qualified leader. So I feel it may be appropriate to choose a young, qualified spiritual leader, also. As with reincarnation, these are different options.

We have discussed this issue within a high-ranking group here in Dharamsala. The key factor must be the will of the Tibetan people. I have already considered a referendum on this question. Everything is possible: a conclave, like in the Catholic Church; a woman as my successor; no Dalai Lama anymore; or perhaps even two, since the Communist Party has given itself the right to be responsible for reincarnations.

I was unanimously asked to make the final decision regarding choosing my successor and how to keep the institution alive. As a Buddhist monk, I am deeply committed to working toward my reincarnation to serve humanity in whatever form or capacity I am most needed. The institution of the Dalai Lama is important only so long as it serves the cause of the Tibetan people.

One thing is clear: that if I am reincarnated as the next Dalai Lama—should that be the best option for the future—it will not be in a China with its present system.

But I hope that there is still plenty of time and that I will have another 10 or even 20 years to think about things. Of course, if we are still in exile then, my successor will presumably have to be found somewhere in India—certainly outside Tibet.

Can the next Dalai Lama be a woman?

HH: There are varied purposes of reincarnation. It is to serve Buddhist Dharma; it is to serve fellow beings. If, for this, the woman form is more effective, then reincarnation should be in the form of a woman.

Would you like to come back as a woman?

HH: Me, personally? I don't know, but the next Dalai Lama reincarnation as a woman is possible. After all, in the Buddhist tradition, in the high reincarnations there have been women, so this is definitely possible.

Do you think you will return to Tibet one day?

HH: I am optimistic that I will be able to return one day. But if I return without a certain degree of freedom, then it is of no use. When the day of my return comes, when a certain measure of pluralism, freedom of opinion, and rule of law has returned to Tibet, I will no longer play a political role or a pronounced spiritual role. I will relinquish all of my historical authority to the local government. We will return the main responsibility to the Tibetans inside Tibet. They know the situation much better, and they have made a lot of effort.

I receive many messages from Tibet—the old say, "Please return before we die," and the young say, "We need you; you should be in a free country." So I remain in exile not as leader but as a free spokesman for the Tibetan people. My real bosses are six million Tibetan people inside Tibet.

ACKNOWLEDGMENTS

The Dalai Lama has offered the world a secular philosophy of universal responsibility that cultivates an altruism bred of an understanding of interdependence, of the myriad ways in which each one of us owes our survival, well-being, and happiness to millions of others. This book has been made possible by the pure, indulgent generosity of spirit, patience, and altruism of His Holiness, who has given of himself and his time to a struggling, ignorant aspirant whose only qualification has been that His Holiness accepted him as a "chela." It remains an eternal prayer—for that seems to offer the only real hope—that I prove worthy of him. It is not enough to express mere gratitude.

The evolution and publishing of this book has been "dependent" on the very qualities His Holiness urges on us, practiced by so many people. My first meeting with His Holiness was facilitated by Tendzin Choegyal, following what seemed then to be a series of coincidences, but I know now were part of some larger design that I am yet to decipher. Rinpoche and his wife, Rinchen Khando la, soon became my Tibetan family, immediately welcoming me and, when I married, my wife into their home. I have usually stayed with them during my visits to Dharamsala to meet His Holiness. I received my first formal initiation from His Holiness, alone, before his personal altar, with Rinpoche, who also served as interpreter and guide. He has been my Dharma Brother

(Guru Bhai!), helping me through many dark nights of the soul. He has ever encouraged and supported me with my writing and work for His Holiness.

Tenzin Geyche Tethong was personal secretary to His Holiness for more than 20 years and retired recently. Tenzin Geyche la served His Holiness with a rare selflessness, great commitment, integrity, and discretion. Till recently, he was the primary contact and facilitator of my personal and formal audiences with His Holiness, often doubling up as translator and interpreter. He and his wife, Chukki la, have been gracious hosts during my visits to their home.

I am grateful to Chhime Rigzing and Tenzin Takhla, who now manage the English section of the Office of His Holiness, for their help and support. Theirs is not an easy task, with the ever-growing demands on His Holiness's time. My thanks to the Office of His Holiness for permission to use extracts from their materials and transcripts.

I first met Tempa Tsering in the early '80s, when he was serving in the Office of His Holiness. His support and enthusiasm for my first project on His Holiness—a documentary film, *Ocean of Wisdom,* for PBS in the U.S.— was invaluable. We stayed in touch intermittently even when he moved out of his official position. In recent years Tempa la has returned to actively serving His Holiness as his representative in Delhi. Working with him again has brought me great joy, encouragement, and support.

My long years of association with the Tibetans and the Foundation for Universal Responsibility of H.H. the Dalai Lama have brought me in touch with numerous Tibetans, from so many of whom I have learnt so much.

I have received great affection and help from them all in my spiritual and samsaric journeys. I wish to particularly acknowledge Lodi Gyari Rinpoche and his wife, Dawa la, and Tashi Wangdin la. I thank Ven. Prof. S. Rinpoche, Ven. Doboom Tulku, and Ven. Lhakdor—the latter for permission to use extracts from materials published by the Library of Tibetan Works & Archives, of which he is the director.

My thanks to Jasjit Purewal for her help in the final restructuring and ordering of the material so that it might read more cogently; to Bindu Badshah for a first edit of the transcribed text; to Shalini Srinivas for collating the vast amount of material; and to Sudha Chandra for her suggestions.

My deep appreciation to my publisher, Ashok Chopra of Hay House India, for his patience and gentle encouragement, not just while reading this book for publication, but for giving me the support and confidence to develop other new ideas. Ratika Kapur at Hay House has been a discreet, meticulous editor and influence on this book.

I am not a professional writer. Without my wife and fellow traveler Meenakshi Gopinath's frequent handholding, I would never have gone down this road. Thank you, Meenu.

— **Rajiv Mehrotra**
Trustee and Secretary
Foundation for Universal Responsibility of
H.H. the Dalai Lama, New Delhi
www. furhhdl.org

THE FOUNDATION FOR
UNIVERSAL RESPONSIBILITY
OF HIS HOLINESS
THE DALAI LAMA

*"To meet the challenges of our times, I believe that
humanity must develop a greater sense of universal
responsibility. Each of us must learn to work not just
for our own individual self, family, or nation, but for
the benefit of all mankind. Today we are so interdependent,
so closely interconnected with each other, that without
a sense of universal responsibility, a feeling of universal
brotherhood and sisterhood, and an understanding and
belief that we really are a part of one big human family,
we cannot hope to overcome the dangers to our very
existence, let alone bring about peace and happiness."*

— His Holiness the Dalai Lama

Mission

- To promote universal responsibility in a
  manner that respects difference and encour-
  ages a diversity of beliefs and practices

- To build a global ethic of nonviolence, co-existence, gender equity, and peace by facilitating processes of personal and social change

- To enrich educational paradigms that tap the transformative potential of the human mind

About the Foundation

The Foundation for Universal Responsibility of His Holiness the Dalai Lama is a not-for-profit, nonsectarian, nondenominational organization established with the Nobel Peace Prize awarded to His Holiness in 1989. In the spirit of the charter of the United Nations, the Foundation brings together men and women of different faiths, professions, and nationalities, through a range of initiatives and mutually sustaining collaborations. The work of the Foundation is global in its reach and transcends nationalist political agendas.

"This Foundation will implement projects to benefit people everywhere, focusing especially on assisting nonviolent methods, on improving communications between religion and science, on securing human rights and democratic freedoms, and on conserving and restoring our precious Mother Earth."

— His Holiness the Dalai Lama

The Vision

- Foster the celebration of diversity; the spirit of universal responsibility; and the understanding of interdependence across faiths, creeds, and religions.

- Support personal transformation in ways that facilitate larger processes of social change.

- Develop and sustain peace-building and coexistence initiatives in regions of violent conflict and social unrest.

- Encourage and cultivate *Ahimsa* (nonviolence) as a guiding principle for interaction among human beings and with their environments.

- Offer inclusive and holistic paradigms of education that prioritize experiential learning, cross-cultural dialogue, and a global ethic of peace and justice.

- Build the capacity for conflict transformation, human rights, and democratic freedom through partnerships with civil society groups across the globe.

- Explore new frontiers for understanding of the mind by building bridges between science and spirituality.

- Support the professional development of future leaders and decision makers through scholarships and fellowships.

- Create media products and educational materials that promote the objectives of the Foundation.

H.H. the Dalai Lama, Chairman
Rajiv Mehrotra, Trustee/Secretary
The Foundation for Universal
Responsibility of H.H. the Dalai Lama
India Habitat Centre, Core 4 A
Lodi Road, New Delhi 110013
India
www.furhhdl.org
Phone: +91-11-2464845

ABOUT THE DALAI LAMA

His Holiness the Dalai Lama (Tenzin Gyatso) is the 14th and current Dalai Lama. Born on July 6, 1935, he was the 5th of 16 children from a farming family in the Tibetan province of Amdo. When he was two years old, he was proclaimed the *tulku* (rebirth) of the 13th Dalai Lama. At the age of 15, he was enthroned as Tibet's Head of State and most important political ruler, as Tibet faced occupation by the forces of the People's Republic of China.

After the collapse of the Tibetan resistance movement in 1959, the Dalai Lama fled to India, where he was active in establishing the Central Tibetan Administration (the Tibetan government in exile) and in seeking to preserve Tibetan culture and education among the thousands of refugees who accompanied him.

A charismatic figure and noted public speaker, His Holiness is the first Dalai Lama to travel to the West. There, he has helped spread Buddhism and promote the concepts of universal responsibility, secular ethics, and religious harmony. In 1989, he was awarded the Nobel Peace Prize for his distinguished writings and his leadership in the resolution of international conflicts, human rights issues, and global environmental problems.

ABOUT RAJIV MEHROTRA

Rajiv Mehrotra has been a personal student of the Dalai Lama for more than 20 years. He's the secretary and a trustee of the Foundation for Universal Responsibility, established by His Holiness the Dalai Lama. He has been a judge for the Templeton Prize for Religion and has addressed plenary sessions of the World Economic Forum, which elected him a Global Leader of Tomorrow. His books include *The Mind of the Guru, Understanding the Dalai Lama,* and *Thakur,* a biography of the mystic Sri Ramakrishna. In addition, he hosts India's longest-running talk show on public television.

We hope you enjoyed this Hay House book. If you'd like to receive a free catalog featuring additional Hay House books and products, or if you'd like information about the Hay Foundation, please contact:

Hay House, Inc.
P.O. Box 5100
Carlsbad, CA 92018-5100

(760) 431-7695 or **(800) 654-5126**
(760) 431-6948 (fax) or **(800) 650-5115 (fax)**
www.hayhouse.com® • **www.hayfoundation.org**

Published and distributed in Australia by: Hay House Australia Pty. Ltd., 18/36 Ralph St., Alexandria NSW 2015 • *Phone:* 612-9669-4299 *Fax:* 612-9669-4144 • www.hayhouse.com.au

Published and distributed in the United Kingdom by: Hay House UK, Ltd., 292B Kensal Rd., London W10 5BE • *Phone:* 44-20-8962-1230 • *Fax:* 44-20-8962-1239 • www.hayhouse.co.uk

Published and distributed in the Republic of South Africa by: Hay House SA (Pty), Ltd., P.O. Box 990, Witkoppen 2068 • *Phone/Fax:* 27-11-467-8904 • orders@psdprom.co.za • www.hayhouse.co.za

Published in India by: Hay House Publishers India, Muskaan Complex, Plot No. 3, B-2, Vasant Kunj, New Delhi 110 070 • *Phone:* 91-11-4176-1620 • *Fax:* 91-11-4176-1630 • www.hayhouse.co.in

Distributed in Canada by: Raincoast, 9050 Shaughnessy St., Vancouver, B.C. V6P 6E5 • *Phone:* (604) 323-7100 *Fax:* (604) 323-2600 • www.raincoast.com

Tune in to **HayHouseRadio.com®** for the best in inspirational talk radio featuring top Hay House authors! And, sign up via the Hay House USA Website to receive the Hay House online newsletter and stay informed about what's going on with your favorite authors. You'll receive bimonthly announcements about Discounts and Offers, Special Events, Product Highlights, Free Excerpts, Giveaways, and more!
www.hayhouse.com®